OWNERSHIP UNLOCKED

MATTHEW F. WILSON

OWNERSHIP UNLOCKED

4 PRINCIPLES
TO BUILD SELF-DRIVEN TEAMS THAT TAKE INITIATIVE, INNOVATE, AND WIN

Published by Brightwave Publishing LLC
www.brightwavepublishing.com
info@brightwavepublishing.com

Cataloging-in-Publication Data is
On file at the Library of Congress

Hardcover ISBN: 979-8-9913571-0-4
E-book ISBN: 979-8-9913571-1-1
Audiobook ISBN: 979-8-9913571-2-8

Get Your FREE Gift and Accelerate Your Success!

Transform Insights into Action Faster!

Readers who use the **Reflection & Quick Action Guide** not only implement the lessons from *Ownership Unlocked* more effectively but also **gain a powerful advantage in transforming their teams.**

Download Your FREE
Reflection & Action Guide Now!

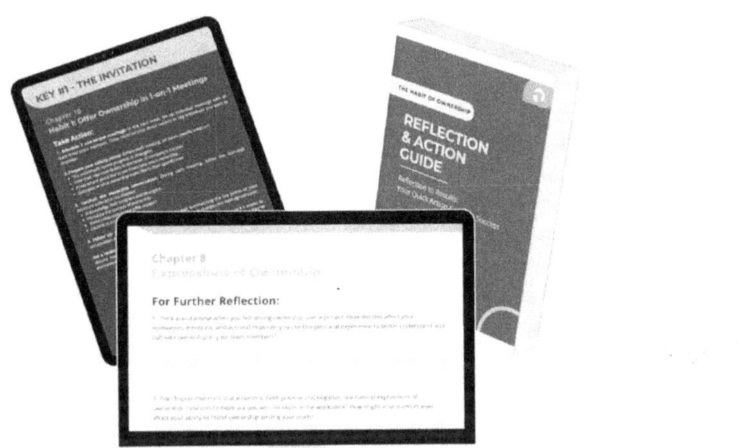

This **40-page, fully editable PDF** includes all the quick action steps from the book, perfect for taking actionable notes on your laptop or tablet.

- **Clarify Your Takeaways**: Capture key insights tailored to your leadership journey.

- **Apply What You Learn Immediately**: Follow step-by-step action items to inspire ownership in your team.

- **Revisit and Reflect Anytime**: Keep all your reflections and strategies in one place, easily accessible whenever you need them.

Get started now by visiting:
OwnershipUnlocked.com/FreeGift

Don't wait—unlock your team's potential today!

To the courageous leaders who understand
that true ownership begins with you.

May these keys unlock the potential
in you and those you lead.

CONTENTS

Introduction: My Story xiii

THE FOUNDATION: WHY OWNERSHIP MATTERS

1   The Transformative Power of Ownership 3

2   Debunking Three Common Ownership Myths 9

3   The 4-Key System for Unlocking Ownership 21

DECODING OWNERSHIP PSYCHOLOGY

4   How to Understand the Psychology of Ownership 31

5   The Bonds of Ownership: Attachment and Identity 39

6   People Own Projects, Not Jobs 45

7   Beliefs That Drive the Ownership Mindset 51

8   How Ownership Transforms Motivation, Emotion, and Behavior 61

KEY #1 – THE INVITATION

9   **Key Concept:** You Must Invite Others to Take Ownership 71

10 How to Ignite Ownership in One-on-Ones 77

11 Why Questions Are More Powerful Than Answers 85

12 The Best Way to Reinforce Ownership Is Through Recognition 91

13 How to Clarify Responsibilities for Maximum Ownership 95

14 Why Collaborative Planning Boosts Collective Ownership 101

KEY #2 – ACCEPTANCE

15 **Key Concept:** Seeing the Good Is Essential for Ownership 111

16 How to Inspire Ownership Through Shared Purpose 117

17 The Best Way to Reframe Work 125

18 How to Connect Team Purpose to Organizational Goals......129

19 Why Success Stories Amplify Ownership......135

20 The Secret to Crafting a Core Credo That Inspires......139

21 The Power of Visualizing Your Mission......143

THE INTERLUDE: MASTERING THE ART OF OWNERSHIP

22 The Importance of Shared Ownership......151

23 Why Extreme Ownership Can Backfire (And How to Avoid It)......157

KEY #3 – INFLUENCE

24 **Key Concept:** Influence Is the Linchpin of Ownership......173

25 Why Micromanaging Kills Ownership (And How to Stop)......179

26 The Surprising Power of Active Listening......191

27 How to Make It Everyone's Problem......199

28 The Best Way to Customize Roles for Maximum Ownership......205

29 Why Flattening Hierarchy Boosts Ownership......213

30 The Secret to Collective Ownership: Goal Setting......219

31 How Giving Budget Control Can Supercharge Ownership......227

KEY #4 – INTENTION

32 **Key Concept:** Why the Future is Vital for Sustained Ownership......237

33 The Secret to Developing People for Long-term Ownership......241

34 How to Reinforce Ownership by Mapping Career Paths......245

35 Why Stay Interviews Are Crucial for Retaining Top Talent......251

CONCLUSION

36 How to Hire for Ownership and Build Your Team of Owners......263

37 The Ultimate Guide to Put the Four Keys into Action......269

APPENDIX: FOR BUSINESS OWNERS

Appendix..281

38 Making Ownership a Company Core Value...............................283

39 The Power of Profit Sharing..285

40 Aligning Interests Through Equity...291

About The Author...299

Acknowledgments...303

Sources...305

My Story

The call that changed my life came in the summer of 2010, when I was offered the opportunity to move across the country and become the product manager for a new suite of digital orthodontic products within Danaher Inc.'s dental division. I would have cross-functional leadership responsibility for an entire product line, not to mention a team of roughly 16 people. I eagerly accepted the opportunity and moved from Baltimore to Los Angeles, California two weeks later.

As I stepped off the airplane at Los Angeles' Burbank airport and saw the rugged San Gabriel mountains towering in the distance, a disturbing question lingered in my mind: *Did I have what it takes to excel in such a big position of leadership?*

Inklings of doubt crept over me.

My first day on the job included a meeting with Oliver Gelles, the marketing vice president who hired me. After the usual pleasantries, I asked him what I would need to do to succeed in my new role. He told me something I will never forget:

"We need someone who will take ownership of the product line, grow it, and bring new products to market."

Time froze in that moment…what did he just say?

Someone who will take ownership. Those words were forever imprinted upon my mind. Mr. Gelles didn't really explain what he meant, but I knew—or at least I thought I knew—what he was asking for. He wanted me to embrace every aspect of this product line as if it were *my own*, to take responsibility for its successes and failures. He wanted me to keep things moving, watch out for roadblocks, and anticipate cost overruns or delays. He needed a leader that would solve problems, regardless of where they came from—whether that be engineering, the supply chain, manufacturing, or somewhere else. In other words, he knew the role demanded someone who would think and act like an owner.

I had been invited to "take ownership" for the first time in my career.

And so I did—perhaps a little too much. It wasn't long before I realized that it's possible to take ownership the wrong way, seeing decisions and responsibilities solely as MINE when, in reality, they were OURS. I was working alongside other "owners," but I failed to recognize it. I took it all on myself, and that blind spot in my leadership led to some rude awakenings—including seriously pissing off the sales team.

But it was also those failures that pushed me to think more deeply about what it really means to take ownership the right way.

Since those early days at Danaher, my understanding of ownership has deepened and evolved. The lessons I learned—both from my successes and mistakes—sparked a curiosity that never faded. I became fascinated with how we, as leaders, can take ownership in the workplace and, just as importantly, how we can inspire others to do the same. When I found myself in a Ph.D. program some years later, that curiously led me to make "psychological ownership" the focus of my research.

For a long time, though, that research remained largely untouched. It wasn't until 2020, when I left Harvard to join a small Christian university, that I began to see the need to turn my academic work into something practical. It was there that I felt a stark shift within myself, as the strong sense of ownership

I had always carried seemed to fade. Within just six months, that ownership spirit seemed to disappear in an environment where initiative was stifled, ambition was discouraged, and a pervasive sense of apathy hung in the air.

I was drowning in a sea of disengagement. Colleagues around me seemed resigned to going through the motions, their passion and drive extinguished. The ethos seemed to be how little one could do and still keep their job. It was a stark reminder of what happens when people lose their sense of ownership at work.

The pain of this experience lit a fire within me. I realized that my academic research on ownership needed to be transformed into something practical that everyday leaders could understand and implement. The popular books I'd read about ownership often fell short of explaining how the psychology of ownership truly works. Those books talked about the importance of getting people to take ownership, but they rarely went beyond platitudes. That's when I realized there was a gap—a disconnect between theory and practical application. I set out to fill that gap by translating the dense academic research on psychological ownership into something that everyday leaders could actually use.

It wasn't easy. The journey from theory to a practical, actionable framework took me almost two years and was often painstaking. But I knew the effort would be worth it. Leaders needed more than vague instructions inspired by great stories— they needed a deep understanding of what actually drives people to take ownership in the first place. That's what I set out to provide.

As I worked on the book, I began hosting workshops with leadership teams to test and refine the concepts. It was through this hands-on experimentation that the *Four Keys to Ownership* framework truly began to take shape—a blend of academic research and real-world application. The feedback from these sessions was both encouraging and validating, and it became clear that the framework was making a meaningful impact.

This book is the culmination of that journey – from corporate curiosity to academic research, through personal struggle and real-world application. The *Four Keys* framework presented here is a hands-on guide to unleashing the power of ownership in any organization. Although I never imagined I would write a book on ownership, I now believe that helping leaders foster a true sense of ownership in their teams is a small part of my calling.

Ownership Unlocked distills my years of corporate experience and academic research into a simple, easy-to-understand guide designed to unlock the ownership mindset within your teams. My hope is that it transforms your business culture and makes leading more rewarding, as you begin working with other "owners" who care as much as you do and are eager to win in business.

- MATTHEW F. WILSON, PH.D.

THE FOUNDATION: WHY OWNERSHIP MATTERS

1

The Transformative Power of Ownership

"The task of leadership is not to put greatness into people, but to elicit it, for the greatness is there already."

\- JOHN BUCHAN, author and former
governor general of Canada

Jeff, a seasoned executive freshly hired from a Fortune 500 pharmaceutical giant, stood in his new office and surveyed his team. The middle-market manufacturing company he joined had ambitious growth plans, but the employees he'd inherited seemed stuck in their ways. They either clung to outdated processes or waited passively for instructions, showing little initiative or investment in their work. As Jeff watched another project fall behind schedule due to a lack of proactive problem-solving, he wrestled with a challenge familiar to leaders at all levels: How do you inspire a sense of ownership among those you lead?

Jeff is not alone in this struggle. Whether you're an emerging leader striving to gain respect, a seasoned manager balancing professional demands with personal life, or an entrepreneur grappling with the realities of payroll, the question of how to foster ownership in your team is likely at the forefront of your mind.

The urgency of this challenge cannot be overstated. In 2023, Gallup estimated that 77 percent of the global workforce was disengaged. Even more alarmingly, Gallup's first quarter 2024 reading of engagement hit an 11-year low in the United States. If people aren't even engaged, they definitely aren't taking ownership of their work. This widespread lack of ownership isn't just a minor inconvenience—it's a crisis that threatens the foundations of organizational success and on the job fulfillment for every leader.

Consider the toll this takes on leaders at every level:

For emerging leaders, a team without ownership means constantly putting out fires instead of focusing on strategic tasks. You find yourself unable to delegate effectively, always feeling one step behind. The promotion you've been eyeing seems to slip further away with each passing day as you struggle to demonstrate your leadership potential.

Seasoned managers often find themselves trapped in a cycle of micromanagement when their team lacks ownership. The stress of being ultimately responsible for a team that doesn't take initiative can be overwhelming. You may feel your career has hit a ceiling, with the next level of leadership seeming unattainable. The work-life balance you've strived for becomes a distant dream as you find yourself continually tied to your job, unable to step away without worrying that everything will fall apart.

For entrepreneurs and business owners, the stakes are even higher. A lack of ownership within your organization can mean the difference between thriving and barely surviving. You may find yourself unable to step away from day-to-day operations, and your dreams of scaling the business seem perpetually out of reach. The joy of financial independence is often marred by the struggle to keep everything afloat—and to meet payroll that runs every two weeks, like clockwork.

But what if there was a way to transform this reality? Imagine a proactive team that not only meets deadlines but anticipates problems before they arise. Picture employees who treat the company's resources as if they were their own, constantly looking for ways to improve efficiency and drive growth. Envision a workplace where innovation thrives because people aren't afraid to take calculated risks or propose new ideas, and everyone wants to win.

This isn't just a pipe dream. It's the reality of teams and organizations where true ownership flourishes. In such environments, leaders at all levels experience a profound shift:

1. Emerging leaders find themselves on an accelerated path to promotion and are able to demonstrate their ability to lead and inspire others.

2. Seasoned managers rediscover their passion for the job and are able to focus on strategic initiatives rather than day-to-day firefighting. They become known for developing high-performing teams, opening doors to even greater leadership opportunities.

3. Entrepreneurs and business owners gain the freedom to focus on scaling their vision and are confident in their team's ability to execute. They can finally press pause, take a step back, and think long-term about their business strategy.

The transformation extends beyond just professional success. Leaders who cultivate ownership find themselves able to maintain a healthier work-life balance. They have better marriages. They take vacations without constant worry. And they enjoy their evenings without endless work-related interruptions, sleeping better at night knowing their team is capable and committed.

But how do we get there? How do we unlock the transformative power of ownership within teams?

This is the question that has driven my research and practice for years. Through my experiences in Fortune 500 companies, academic research (including a Ph.D. focused on psychological ownership and working at Harvard's Human Flourishing Program), and consulting work with numerous leaders, I've developed a framework that can help you cultivate a culture of ownership in your organization.

In this book, we'll explore four principles that I call the Four Keys to Ownership: Invitation, Acceptance, Influence, and Intention. These keys, when properly understood and applied, can unlock the potential within your team, transforming not just your organization's performance, but your experience as a leader.

The Invitation Key will show you how to effectively extend the crucial invitation to ownership, inspiring your team to go above and beyond their prescribed duties.

The Acceptance Key will help you understand the psychological triggers that make people embrace ownership, even in roles they previously found uninspiring.

The Influence Key will teach you how to empower your team without losing control, fostering an environment where innovation and problem-solving become second nature.

The Intention Key will provide strategies to reduce turnover and foster long-term commitment, so you can build a team that's invested in the organization's future.

This isn't just theory. Throughout the book, you'll find real-world examples of how these keys have been applied in various leadership contexts. You'll see how Jeff and leaders like him have used these principles to transform their teams and their own leadership experiences.

The journey to creating a culture of ownership isn't always easy. It requires patience, persistence, and a willingness to change our own leadership habits. But the rewards—both for you as a leader and for your organization—are great.

As we delve into each of the Four Keys, you'll learn practical strategies and develop new habits that will help you inspire ownership at every level of your organization. You'll discover how to invite your team members to take ownership, help them accept the responsibility that comes with it, give them the influence they need to truly own their work, and finally, foster their intention to stay and grow with your organization.

Whether you're in Jeff's position, inheriting a team set in its ways, or you're looking to take your high-performing team to the next level, the principles in this book will guide you. They are the fundamental building blocks of creating a culture where ownership thrives.

In today's business world, cultivating ownership isn't just a nice-to-have—it's a necessity if you want to grow. Every day you delay is a day the competition adapts and pulls ahead, or you get behind in your career. But with the *Four Keys to Ownership*, you have the blueprint to not just compete, but to excel in any business environment.

I must admit, however, that my mission in writing this book goes beyond the success of you and your organization. I care about your people, and I want them to thrive too. When you learn to lead for ownership, you also learn how to care well for those who work for you. In fact, one of the best ways to love your people is to empower and inspire them to do their greatest work. By encouraging them to show up every day with an ownership mindset, you are giving them one of the greatest gifts leaders can give: a profound sense of purpose and fulfillment at work, which not only elevates their performance but also enriches their overall happiness and well-being.

Are you ready to unlock the full potential of your team? To transform your leadership journey from one of constant struggle to one of strategic impact? To finally build the organization you've always dreamed of?

Then it's time to turn the page and unlock the transformative power of ownership. Your journey begins now.

2

Debunking Three Common Ownership Myths

"Leaders become great, not because of their power,
but because of their ability to empower others."

- John C. Maxwell, author of *The*
Five Levels of Leadership

The job of a great leader is to get the right people on the bus, argues author and researcher Jim Collins in his bestselling book *Good to Great*.[1] He emphasizes that great companies focus first on getting the right people on the bus (and the wrong people off the bus) before figuring out where to drive. While there is truth to this principle, it's not the whole story. In fact, this kind of claim can be misleading.

Collin's leadership principle, if oversimplified, can lead to dangerous misconceptions about ownership in the workplace. To avoid those misconceptions and truly understand ownership, we must debunk three prevalent myths:

Myth #1: Ownership is a personality trait.

Myth #2: Ownership, responsibility, and accountability are all the same thing.

---

[1]   James C. Collins, *Good to Great: Why Some Companies Make the Leap ... and Others Don't*, 1st ed., Business Book Summary (New York, NY: HarperBusiness, 2001).

Myth #3: Employees must have a legal or financial stake in your company to experience psychological ownership.

By addressing these myths head-on, we'll pave the way for a deeper understanding of how to cultivate genuine ownership in your organization. Let's examine each of these myths in turn, starting with the most pervasive one.

MYTH #1:
OWNERSHIP IS A PERSONALITY TRAIT

It's tempting to believe that some people are natural "owners" while others simply aren't, but this assumption overlooks a crucial factor: the power of environment. Your people have been conditioned by your organization, its leaders, and your company's culture, which includes its management style. That's not to mention, of course, all the previous managers and companies they've worked for. If someone's not taking ownership, it's rarely a personality problem; it's more likely that the natural human propensity to take ownership has been beaten out of them. When we ascribe someone's lack of ownership to a personality problem, it's easy to falsely conclude that the right course of action is to weed out this "bad apple" instead of looking in the mirror—both at our own leadership and at the leadership of our organization.

We think to ourselves that if we just had the right people on the bus, we could go the distance.

If only it were that easy.

The truth is that when your leadership style or organization's culture disables ownership, you could replace your entire team with the very best talent out there and still end up back in the same place. Now hear me carefully, please: I'm not arguing that continual underperformance should be tolerated, or that you shouldn't carefully consider who gets on your bus. Good hiring practices are essential to every organization. But I want to persuade you that your first assumption about everyone ought to be that they are capable of eagerly taking ownership in their work—*if* they are given the chance.

Research has shown us that having a sense of ownership in our work is a natural and normal psychological state. Human beings are hardwired to develop a sense of ownership whenever we invest our time, effort, and creativity into something, especially our work. In fact, a sense of ownership starts expressing itself early in life—it can even be seen in 18-month-old children.[2]

To help you see this, imagine yourself in a remote, medieval forest. You are there with only a few other people and have just a backpack's worth of supplies. You need shelter, so you head into the woods to chop down some trees and build yourself a house (yes, there was an ax in your backpack). You spend several weeks working on it, and when it's finished, the most natural and normal thing in the world is for you to experience a strong sense of ownership over the house—your new creation.

"That's mine!" you will say.

Ownership is such a basic part of our psychology that most people don't even question it. But why is it, exactly, that you would feel such a strong sense of ownership over this house? If you think about it, you didn't make those trees or vines, or the mud you used, now did you? You were not their creator. God or the universe was. All you did was mold, assemble, and shape something that was already there—and yet, you claim the shelter as "yours."

John Locke was a British philosopher who puzzled over this question of ownership a great deal, doing many thought experiments similar to this one. He was searching for the

---

[2] Philippe Rochat, *Origins of Possession: Owning and Sharing in Development* (Cambridge: Cambridge University Press, 2014).

foundations and origins of private property, but what he discovered was an insight about ownership psychology—namely, that human beings *naturally* form strong psychological ties to things once we "mix our labor" into them. These things, at least in our own minds, become "mine" and "ours," whether we have any real right to them or not.[3]

There are big differences between building log houses and participating in the modern workforce. One reason that modern workers often struggle to maintain their natural sense of ownership is that every organization intentionally disables ownership at least in some ways. The very nature of being an "organization" means that a tension exists between processes and procedures designed to ensure productivity and quality and the freedom desired by all workers to express agency within their work.

In other words, organizations take away some aspects of individual psychological ownership in order to be more efficient and effective as a whole. The key for leaders is to exercise self-awareness about the ways you and your organization are (and are not) supporting a culture of ownership among the parts of that whole. A high level of self-awareness is one of the many leadership skills this book will help you develop.

What does this all mean for you? Instead of dismissing employees as inherently lacking ownership, examine the work environment you've created. Are you providing opportunities for ownership? Are you recognizing and rewarding ownership behaviors? By shifting your focus from the individual to the environment, you open up new possibilities for fostering ownership across your entire team.

---

[3] John Locke, *Two Treatises of Government*, ed. L. A. Selby-Bigge (Oxford: Clarendon Press, 1739).

MYTH #2:
OWNERSHIP, RESPONSIBILITY, AND ACCOUNTABILITY ARE ALL THE SAME THING.

Many management books discuss the importance of accountability and how to create systems that will keep people accountable. Those systems can be very good, and the ability to hold people accountable is certainly a necessary skill for all leaders. But it's possible for employees to be both responsible and accountable, yet still not take ownership in their work.

Responsible employees show up on time. They leave punctually. They do what they're told. If you give responsible employees a to-do list, they will get it done. These are good employees, but something is missing. When people operate merely from a sense of responsibility, they usually do what they're told to do—but nothing more. One might also notice the absence of passion behind their work, meaning that the personal and emotional investment is just not there. They don't think, feel, or act like owners.

As you read this book, then, please remember that when I talk about ownership, it is not a synonym for "responsibility" or "accountability." These are related concepts, but they are distinct.

The truth is ownership goes beyond responsibility and accountability. It's the umbrella concept under which these concepts fall, but it reaches further. When people truly take ownership, they don't just responsibly do what they're told or accept blame when things go wrong. They invest themselves in their work. They think proactively and drive innovation.

What does this mean for you? As you read on, you'll discover that fostering ownership isn't about implementing new systems or finding clever ways to motivate your team. Instead, get ready to gain insights into why people naturally want to take ownership and how you can nurture that instinct. This book isn't about finding new ways to push your team from the outside. It's about creating an environment where ownership thrives on its own.

By the end, you'll have practical tools to transform how your team approaches their work. You'll be able to foster a culture where people don't just complete tasks—they own outcomes. And in the process, you'll become the kind of leader who inspires true ownership, not just compliance.

MYTH #3:
EMPLOYEES MUST HAVE A LEGAL OR FINANCIAL STAKE IN YOUR COMPANY TO EXPERIENCE PSYCHOLOGICAL OWNERSHIP.

Many leaders assume that true ownership only comes with equity, but the reality is far more nuanced and powerful. The truth is that having legal or financial ownership is not necessary, nor is it sufficient, when aiming to evoke a sense of psychological ownership. We know it's not necessary because many people experience a deep sense of psychological ownership without ever having any formal or legal ownership rights. We see this every day. For example, people take ownership of their volunteer work for churches, nonprofit organizations, and the many projects they undertake with family members at home. Even without a legal or financial stake, we can develop an ownership mindset that is strong and active.

Possessing legal ownership (i.e., equity) is also not sufficient when trying to inspire attitudes of psychological ownership. The mere act of granting someone equity or ownership in your company does not guarantee they will suddenly feel invested in their work. Organizations that create stock option plans or employee stock ownership plans (ESOPs) often hope this will be the case[4] but quickly discover otherwise. Research shows that granting equity to employees is helpful, but it does not guarantee that people will start experiencing psychological ownership in their work.[5] If you don't believe me, just consider retirement portfolios. People may legally "own" these assets, yet they tend to have very little interest in them and no active involvement or sense of ownership in the day-to-day operations of those companies.

If psychological ownership doesn't automatically come from legal or financial ownership, how does it occur?

Psychological ownership arises from the emotional investment in, and personal identification with, our work—in other words, we experience the work as becoming a part of ourselves.[6] It becomes "OURS." The ownership mindset must arise from within. It can't be imposed by signed legal documents, stock shares, or managerial demands. Psychological ownership requires an alignment of a person's perceptions, beliefs, and attachments to their work, so that it becomes MINE in both the heart and mind.

In the Appendix, I discuss how offering legal ownership through an equity incentive plan can augment other leadership strategies to cultivate ownership. For now, though, I want to make sure it's clear that legal and psychological ownership are distinct, and that one is not necessary or sufficient for the other.

Why is debunking this myth so important? Even if you work at a company that does not offer equity to employees, you can still lead for ownership and inspire the ownership mindset on

---

4   Corey Rosen, *Beyond Engagement: How to Make Your Business an Idea Factory* (National Center for Employee Ownership, 2020).

5   Rosen.

6   Jon L. Pierce, Tatiana Kostova, and Kurt T. Dirks, "Toward a Theory of Psychological Ownership in Organizations," *The Academy of Management Review* 26, no. 2 (2001): 298–310; Jon L. Pierce, Tatiana Kostova, and Kurt T. Dirks, "The State of Psychological Ownership: Integrating and Extending a Century of Research," *Review of General Psychology* 7, no. 1 (2003): 84–107.

your teams. If you're an executive or business owner, you can't rely solely on financial incentives or legal ownership structures to foster a sense of ownership. You'll need to complement equity incentives with a management environment that supports people developing a psychological connection to their work. This might involve giving them more autonomy, involving them in decision-making processes, or helping them see the direct impact of their work on the company's success and its customers.

Now that we've cleared away these common misconceptions, let's lay the groundwork for a deeper understanding of ownership. This is only a preview, and we'll unpack these concepts more as we go, but I want to start introducing them to lay the groundwork for future chapters. Here they are:

Ownership Is a Type of Attachment. Throughout the book, I will discuss psychological ownership in terms of attachment. Human beings form psychological attachments (or bonds) to many different things. We form attachments to our parents, children, extended family, friends, and even to certain places or objects that are familiar to us.[7] Just think of the connections you have with a favorite restaurant, park, or even a coffee cup. "Ownership" represents just one particular type of human attachment. Other well-researched attachment types include love and place attachments.

---

[7] Leila Scannell and Robert Gifford, "Defining Place Attachment: A Tripartite Organizing Framework," *Journal of Environmental Psychology* 30 (2010): 1–10; Roy F. Baumeister and Mark R. Leary, "The Need to Belong: Desire for Interpersonal Attachments as a Fundamental Human Motivation," *Psychological Bulletin* 117, no. 3 (1995): 497–529, https://doi.org/10.1037/0033-2909.117.3.497; Maria Vittoria Giuliani, "Theory of Attachment and Place Attachment," in *Psychological Theories for Environmental Issues* (Aldershot: Ashgate, 2003), 137–70; Edward Harcourt, "Attachment Theory, Character, and Naturalism," in *Aristotelian Ethics in Contemporary Perspective*, ed. Julia Peters, Routledge Studies in Ethics and Moral Theory 21 (New York: Routledge, 2013), 145–57.

Ownership Requires Self-Identification. Taking ownership in our work stems from an investment of our time, energy, and creativity—our very selves—into the work we do. Psychological ownership therefore involves a kind of self-identification with our projects, at least to a degree. To see something as MINE means that I see something of myself in it, and something of it in myself.

Common Ownership is Essential. *Exclusive* psychological ownership is when I see work solely as MINE and belonging to no one else. *Common* ownership means that I recognize that there are other "owners" involved, and I see the work as both MINE *and* OURS. When we take ownership in common, we recognize and appreciate that other people contribute to the success and outcomes of our projects—that they are co-owners. As a leader, it's your job to ensure that people on your team (including you!) don't get too possessive of the work, and that everyone maintains a strong sense of "WE" and "OURS."

Ownership Mindsets Are Cultivated. Mindsets exist when our beliefs and perceptions function as a lens through which we see the world. Mindsets formed at work are the result of a variety of factors. For example, our mindset may depend on whether we see our work as being valued by senior leaders, whether we think it's worthwhile, and what we believe about the influence and impact we have on our projects. These factors all contribute to a work mindset that acts as a filter for our daily experiences. Cultivating an ownership mindset in your employees may require changing their beliefs and perceptions about their work and how it contributes to the organization.

As we delve deeper into these concepts, you'll discover how they form the foundation of the *Four Keys to Ownership* framework. These Keys will equip you to unlock genuine psychological ownership within your team. By applying the Keys, you'll help each team member identify with a common project, become attached to it as owner, and work together with others under the shared sense of "OURS." Let's learn more about the Four Keys in the next chapter.

3

The 4-Key System for Unlocking Ownership

"Ownership is the most powerful weapon a team can have."

- Patricia Summitt, women's basketball
coach at the University of Tennessee

The *Four Keys to Ownership* framework began to materialize in the summer of 2022, as my longtime friend and business partner, Dan, and I prepared to host a management workshop on ownership. We locked ourselves in a conference room for two days, using lots of easel paper and multicolored markers to map it all out. My academic research had highlighted the principles of psychological ownership—now, I just needed a way to organize and present it clearly.

Soon, it became apparent that the principles of psychological ownership could be boiled down into four simple "Keys." Each Key was a necessary component of psychological ownership, and if one wanted to "unlock" the ownership mindset, all of them needed to be "turned." The Keys are:

1) **Invitation.** You must invite your employees to take ownership in their work.

2) **Acceptance**. People must accept your offer of ownership.

3) **Influence**. People must genuinely perceive that they have influence over their projects.

21

4) Intention. People must intend to remain at their projects if they are going to take ownership in them.

Although much of this framework came out over the course of two days, it didn't emerge in a vacuum. It's the product of years of academic research, including my Ph.D. work on psychological ownership, combined with decades of hands-on experience in Fortune 500 companies and consulting with industry leaders. Dan himself has been a leadership coach for over two decades. The Four Keys represent a distillation of complex psychological principles into actionable leadership strategies.

To help explain the concept behind each Key, let me share a parable that illustrates how the *Four Keys to Ownership* framework unlocks ownership psychology:

> A boy is about to turn sixteen years old. His dad wants to buy him a car as a present, so he goes to the dealer, picks one out, and purchases it. He titles and registers the car in his son's name, so that on the date of purchase his son has full *legal* ownership of it.
>
> But the dad doesn't give it to him yet. He waits until his son's birthday. When the day arrives, the son comes home from school to find the car waiting in the driveway. The boy smiles from ear to ear as his dad joyously hands him the keys. Together, they take it for a spin.
>
> Over the next several weeks and months, the dad regularly sees his son out washing the car, putting tire-black on the wheels, and even doing his own oil changes. The dad notices that his son has fully "taken ownership" (psychologically) of the car that he already (legally) owned.

Although it's a simple story, it illustrates the four psychological Keys at work, all of which are all necessary for someone to take psychological ownership. Let's unpack them together.

The first Key is rather obvious, although it's easily and often overlooked in many business contexts. I call it the Invitation. The dad tells his son that the car is his gift. In this way, he invites his son to take ownership. This invitation must be made before the son can even consider taking ownership of the car from a psychological perspective. Remember, he is *already* the legal owner. The other part of this invitation, or course, is the physical act of handing over the keys.

The second Key to ownership is Acceptance. The son must be willing to accept this car *as his own*. We can easily imagine scenarios where the son might *not* accept the car. If he and his dad had a contentious relationship, for example, he might refuse to accept anything associated with his dad. Or, if the son didn't like the look of the car, he might feel embarrassed and reject it for that reason. For anyone to accept something as their own, *they must perceive it as a good thing*. If they do not, they won't be willing or able to become attached as an owner.

The third Key is Influence. Influence is about our sense of agency, and it is at the heart of ownership psychology. In order for the son to take ownership and *retain* that mindset of ownership over time, he must perceive that he has real influence and some control over the car. In other words, he must have the power to drive it when and where he wants, at least most of the time. If he needs his dad's permission every time he wants to use it, or if he is constantly being told that he cannot go here or there, then his sense of ownership diminishes. His legal ownership of the car no longer matters, psychologically speaking. Without the son having some degree of autonomy, the car will still, practically, belong to his dad. Central to the psychology of ownership is that an owner must be able to control, direct, or influence the target of ownership in some way.

Finally, the fourth Key is Intention. In order for the son to retain his sense of ownership, he must intend to use the car in the future. He must see the car as worth having and maintaining for his future use. That is one reason why he washes and maintains it so well. Without this intention, he would have little reason or motivation to perform such tasks.

To appreciate the importance of this last Key, imagine a scenario where the son's family moves to New York City. What if he now no longer has the need for the car? Although he might put it in storage and retain *legal* ownership of it, as soon as he stops intending to use the car, he will become mentally and emotionally detached. He will no longer take *psychological* ownership. This detachment is similar to a business owner who plans to retire and is no longer involved in day-to-day operations. Although he retains legal ownership, and he might be concerned that it produces a profit, he no longer "takes ownership" in it from a psychological perspective. People only take ownership in projects when they intend to continue participating in their future.

Let's quickly review.

The Invitation Key is about explicitly offering ownership. In the car story, it's the act of giving the keys. The Acceptance Key involves the recipient embracing ownership. The son accepts the car as his own. The Influence Key is about having real control or impact. The son needs to be able to (mostly) drive the car as he wishes. The Intention Key relates to future involvement. The son intends to keep and maintain the car and use it in the future.

If any one of the Keys goes missing, the son in our story would stop taking psychological ownership of the car, even if he retained legal ownership. The *Four Keys to Ownership* work together at a high level to produce a full sense of ownership. We'll discuss in more depth the psychology behind these Keys in the next section. But first, let me provide a roadmap to what else lies ahead.

WHAT'S AHEAD

This book is organized so that you can learn how to lead for ownership by implementing the *Four Keys to Ownership* framework. Each section is broken into short chapters, which correspond to that section's theme.

In Section 2, I teach you the fundamentals of ownership psychology. This section gives you a robust picture of what occurs, on a psychological level, when people take ownership at work. You'll discover why some team members seem naturally driven while others appear apathetic. These principles are important for you to understand because they ground everything else in the sections that follow.

The remaining sections are dedicated to each Key of Ownership. The psychological principles behind each Key may be simple, but the challenge is how to put those Keys into practice. Each section begins with a chapter that delves deeper into the "key concept" or psychological principle behind the Key, beyond the overview just provided. The chapters that follow the key concept chapter discuss specific leadership practices that make the psychological principle tangible and actionable in your leadership. They represent ways of "turning" the Keys to unlock a sense of ownership in your people.

For senior and experienced leaders, some of these practices may be familiar, and I hope you already employ many of them. My challenge for you is to review them with fresh eyes, examining them in yourself and in those you lead. Try to appreciate the significance of the practice in how you can better lead for ownership.

For newer and less experienced leaders, we cover a lot of ground in this book. The are many leadership practices that can impact ownership and the Four Keys. Don't worry. To be successful, you don't have to master all of them—you will, however, want to apply some of the practices and habits from each Key. I will show you how to do this at the end of the book.

Section 3 is about Key #1: Invitation. How do you inspire someone to take ownership when they've been conditioned not to? You'll learn how to extend invitations that ignite ownership, even in the most reluctant team members.

Section 4 covers Key #2: Acceptance. Ever had a team member who just couldn't see the value in their work? Learn how to guide your team in accepting projects as their own, transforming routine tasks into meaningful contributions. You'll explore techniques to connect individual work to the bigger picture, making even the most routine tasks feel significant.

Section 5 provides an Interlude. This material is so important that we will pause our discussion of the Keys in order to reflect on what it means to take ownership well. The two chapters in this section present ways that taking ownership can go wrong. On the one hand, one can err by seeing work projects as only MINE, and not OURS. This is a problem that produces an unhealthy degree of possessiveness.

On the other hand, someone can become too attached to their work by the degree to which they identify with it. This can negatively affect overall well-being and, ultimately, an employee's performance. "Extreme ownership" presents real dangers. In these chapters, I introduce the idea that taking ownership *well* is a kind of virtue—a middle way between two extremes.

Section 6 returns to the earlier rhythm of our discussion with Key #3: Influence. How do you give your team real influence without losing control? You'll gain strategies to empower your team while maintaining strategic direction.

Section 7 discusses the final Key: Intention. How do you keep your best talent from walking out the door? Learn to cultivate long-term commitment using three ownership-ready retention strategies.

At the end of each chapter, I provide questions for further reflection or quick action steps to take, depending on whether the chapter is more theoretical or practical. I encourage you to answer these questions and start taking action as you progress. That said, the final chapter is the place where we'll pull it all together. This chapter provides you with resources and a methodology for how to take next steps. You'll develop a plan unique to you, because it will be the product of a team audit and a short self-assessment.

As you journey through these Keys, you'll not only become a more effective leader but also gain insights that can transform your personal relationships. The principles of ownership apply beyond the workplace—they can make you a better parent, spouse, and friend by deepening your understanding of human psychology and motivation.

And finally, a word of exhortation before we jump in: although this book is written from the perspective of how you can inspire a sense of ownership *in those you lead*, I invite you to take a look at yourself and how you show up as an "owner." To create a sense of ownership among your teams, you must lead by example.

Are you ready? Let's dive in.

DECODING OWNERSHIP PSYCHOLOGY

4

How to Understand the Psychology of Ownership

"We are what we repeatedly do. Excellence, then, is not an act, but a habit."

- WILL DURANT, author of *The Story of Philosophy*

Picture this: Adam, a cost accountant at a fish packaging company, discovers an error in the frozen fish division's financial reports. It's not his fault, but instead of shrugging it off, he feels compelled to fix it. He tracks down the responsible financial accountant, and together, they stay several hours after work to identify the root cause and correct the report. As Adam leaves work that night, he feels a deep sense of relief and pride. He's also genuinely grateful to his coworker for staying late to help.

Fast forward a month. Adam overhears the frozen fish team lamenting lost shelf space at Costco due to uncompetitive pricing. The key account manager insists they're already selling at or near cost. Something doesn't sit right with Adam. He decides to dig deeper.

On his own initiative, Adam dives into their cost procedures and meets with manufacturing personnel. His persistence pays off. By adjusting some excessive cost allocations, he uncovers a way to reduce the product's manufacturing cost. Excited, he shares his solution with the sales team, enabling them to lower prices and regain their competitive edge.

Adam's manager is thrilled with his proactive problem-solving and dedication to serving customers. His actions create a sense of teamwork and solidarity among his colleagues. Adam exemplifies what it means to take ownership at work.

Now, you might be thinking, "That's great, but what does Adam's story really tell me?" Let's break it down.

Adam's story isn't merely about a dedicated employee going above and beyond. It's a window into the psychology of ownership at work. When Adam discovered the initial error, he felt personally invested in fixing it, even though it wasn't his direct responsibility. That's ownership. When he heard about the pricing issue, he took it upon himself to investigate and find a solution. Again, ownership in action.

But it goes deeper than just actions. Remember how Adam felt relieved and proud after fixing the initial error? Those emotions are key indicators of psychological ownership. He was emotionally invested in the outcome. His gratitude towards his coworker who stayed late? That's a sign of seeing the project as a shared responsibility, as OURS—another aspect of healthy ownership.

Adam's story illustrates several characteristics of someone with a strong sense of psychological ownership:

- Personal investment beyond formal job duties
- Proactive problem-solving
- Emotional connection to outcomes
- Intrinsic motivation to contribute
- Seeing issues as "our problem" rather than "someone else's problem"

As we dive deeper into the psychology of ownership, keep Adam's story in mind. We'll refer back to it as we explore the key components that drive this powerful mindset.

Each chapter in this Section on decoding ownership psychology will break down the key components underlying the mindset. We'll examine how people's perceptions, beliefs, identifications, and attachments interact to generate the attitudes and behaviors Adam displayed. Understanding these psychological drivers is essential for growing your ability to lead for ownership and, ultimately, for helping you grow and scale your business.

A MODEL OF PSYCHOLOGICAL OWNERSHIP

To fully understand what drives the ownership psychology, we must unpack some foundational psychological concepts.[8] These concepts shed light on how different parts of our psychology converge to generate ownership attitudes and behaviors.

---

[8] In management psychology literature, psychological ownership was first defined by Pierce et al. in their seminal 2001 paper. Since then, the field has bloomed. See: Pierce, Kostova, and Dirks, "Toward a Theory of Psychological Ownership in Organizations"; Jon L. Pierce and Iiro Jussila, *Psychological Ownership and the Organizational Context* (Northampton, MA: Edward Elgar Publishing, 2011); Linn Van Dyne and Jon L. Pierce, "Psychological Ownership and Feelings of Possession: Three Field Studies Predicting Employee Attitudes and Organizational Citizenship Behavior.," *Journal of Organizational Behavior* 25 (2004): 439–359; James B. Avey et al., "Psychological Ownership: Theoretical Extensions, Measurement and Relation to Work Outcomes," *Journal of Organizational Behavior* 30, no. 2 (2009): 173–91; Sarah Dawkins et al., "Psychological Ownership: A Review and Research Agenda," *Journal of Organizational Behavior* 38 (2017): 163–83; Fabian Bernhard and Michael O'Driscoll, "Psychological Ownership in Small Family-Owned Businesses: Leadership Style and Nonfamily-Employees' Work Attitudes and Behaviors," *Group and Organization Management* 36, no. 3 (2011): 345–84; Joann Peck and Webb Luangrath Andrea, "Looking Ahead: Future Research in Psychological Ownership," in *Psychological Ownership and Consumer Behavior*, ed. Joann Peck and Suzanne Shu (Springer, 2018); Melissa G. Mayhew et al., "A Study of the Antecedents and Consequences of Psychological Ownership in Organizational Settings," *The Journal of Social Psychology* 147, no. 5 (2007): 477–500.

The model below illustrates the process of how psychological ownership develops and manifests. Let's break it down:

Figure 4.1

THE PSYCHOLOGY OF OWNERSHIP

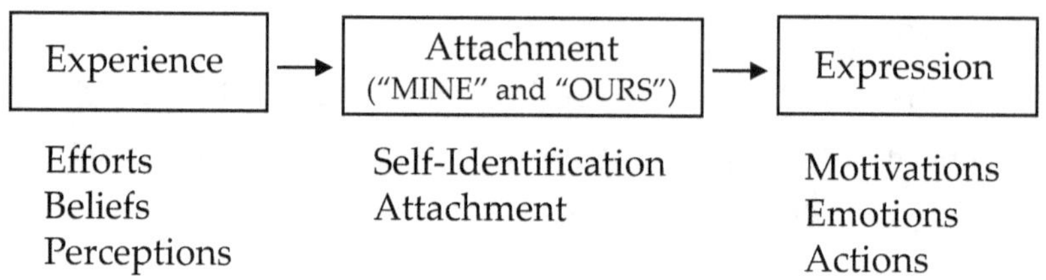

The box on the left represents an employee's experience going to work. Beyond merely the effort they put into their job, it also includes the beliefs and perceptions that they form about work and about their company as a whole. These include perceptions on whether their work is valued, what impact their work has on the company's success, and whether they have a long-term future at the company. A large network of beliefs and perceptions forms as an employee experiences the company's culture and what it's like to work there—including experiences with their boss, other colleagues, and senior leadership. Collectively, these experiences function as the input to the model.

The middle box represents an employee's attachment to their individual work projects. When the experiences an employee has (in the left box) support a sense of ownership, they will start to see work projects under the aspect of being *MINE* and *OURS* (the middle box). The employee develops an attachment and begins to identify with their work. In other words, projects become an extension of the self. This is what I call *the ownership attachment*.

The right-hand box represents the various expressions of psychological ownership. These expressions include an employee's motivations, emotions, and actions related to their work projects.

These can vary dramatically depending on whether or not the employee has developed an ownership attachment.

Let's return our attention to the middle part of the model, the box labeled "attachment." This part needs the most explaining.

The core of psychological ownership is whether a person "sees" or construes a common project as MINE and OURS, or whether they simply see it as "required action." It is most helpful to understand this through two psychological mechanisms: the lenses of *attachment* and *identification*.

(i) *Attachment.* Attachments are psychological "bonds" that human beings form with other people, places, things, and projects. As we act within a project and extend our agency to it, we often become psychologically attached.[9]

(ii) *Identification.* We identify ourselves with our work when we see something of ourselves in the work being reflected back to us. To some extent and at varying degrees, our work becomes part of our identity: our conception of ourselves.[10]

The concepts of attachment and identification partially explain what it means to see a project as "MINE," at least in the ownership sense. When a person takes ownership, their work projects become part of their identity and are seen as an extension of the self. The less a person identifies with a project, the less they see it as their own.

Seeing a project as MINE and OURS is therefore something that happens on a continuum. We do this to different degrees at different times. Sometimes, we feel more attached to our work. Other times, it feels like less of a part of who we are.

---

[9] Pierce, Kostova, and Dirks, "Toward a Theory of Psychological Ownership in Organizations."

[10] Van Dyne and Pierce, "Psychological Ownership and Feelings of Possession: Three Field Studies Predicting Employee Attitudes and Organizational Citizenship Behavior."

If a person is completely detached and does not identify with a project *at all*, then—by definition—they are not experiencing psychological ownership. Factory workers who merely push a button all day are a good example of this. They typically feel detached from their work. Karl Marx and others have rightly described this condition as "alienation" from one's work and criticized it as being unnatural or inhuman.[11] In this condition, workers spend their time and energy on work they feel completely divorced from.[12]

At the same time, an extremely high degree of attachment to one's work is not necessarily a good thing, either. Finding an optimal level of work attachment is healthiest, both for well-being and optimal performance. We'll talk about this more in Section 5, when we discuss how to take ownership correctly.

Think back to Adam's story. His attachment to his work was evident in how he took initiative beyond his job description. His identification showed in the way he saw the company's challenges as his own to solve. These bonds of ownership—attachment and identity—are crucial to understanding how psychological ownership develops and manifests in the workplace.

But how exactly do these bonds form? What makes us identify so strongly with our work that it becomes an extension of ourselves? And how can we, as leaders, foster these connections without pushing our teams into unhealthy over-attachment?

In the next chapter, we dive deeper into the nature of these psychological bonds. We'll explore how attachment and identity shape how we relate to people and things outside of ourselves, and why they're so fundamental to the concept of ownership.

---

[11] István Mészáros, *Marx's Theory of Alienation* (London: Merlin Press, 1970). Karl Marx is often credited as being the founder of the communist movement.

[12] Rahel Jaeggi, *Alienation*, ed. Frederick Neuhouser, trans. Frederick Neuhouser and Alan E. Smith (New York: Columbia University Press, 2014).

Understanding these mechanisms will provide you with valuable insights into how you can cultivate ownership on your team, setting the stage for the practical strategies we'll discuss later in the book.

So, let's turn the page and dive into the fascinating world of attachment and identity. It's time to explore the deep psychological roots of ownership.

For Further Reflection

1. How does Adam's story illustrate the difference between merely taking responsibility and truly embodying psychological ownership? Can you identify similar examples in your own organization?

2. Reflect on a time when you felt a strong sense of ownership in your work. How did your experience align with the psychological ownership model presented in this chapter?

3. The chapter discusses how seeing a project as MINE and OURS occurs on a continuum. In your current role, where do you think your team members fall on this continuum? What factors might influence their position?

5

The Bonds of Ownership: Attachment and Identity

"Success isn't guaranteed, but failure is certain if you aren't truly emotionally invested in your work."

- CHRISTOPHER ISAAC "BIZ" STONE,
co-founder of Twitter

Have you ever felt proud of someone you loved—perhaps a child, spouse, or other family member? I'll never forget the pride I felt when my three-year-old son, Roy, rode his bike for the very first time. He tried to ride without training wheels several times before, but each time he got on his bike, he would soon get off again. He said he was too scared.

I was patient and waited several weeks before asking him if he wanted to try again. This time, I could sense something was different. He had a look of determination in his eye. He was ready. We got him started pedaling, and I ran beside him. Then, *voilà*! I took my hand off the back of his seat, and he was riding on his own! My wife and two other kids watched and cheered. After about 15 yards, Roy stopped and smiled from ear to ear, and I could not have been prouder.

Have you ever experienced something like this? If you have ever felt pride for someone else's accomplishment, then you have experienced an emotion that is a result of self-identification.[13]

If you think about it, feeling proud about what someone else does is kind of strange. Why should *you* feel proud for something that wasn't your achievement? Pride is normally a self-reflexive emotion. We feel proud about our *own* achievements and the things for which *we* are responsible.

My son riding his bike for the first time wasn't my accomplishment. It was his. I already know how to ride a bike. My experience of pride was only possible because of how I *identify* with and am *attached* to him. I recognize something of myself in my son.

I don't feel pride when other three-year-olds ride their bikes for the first time. Imagine my business partner Dan were to call and tell me that his son rode a bike. I might respond with, "Wow, that's great," and maybe I'd feel happy for him. More likely, I'd wonder, "Why are you telling me this?" Either way, I wouldn't feel pride.

The reason I felt proud about my son's accomplishment was because he is MY son. I identify with him as an extension of myself. He is part of me, psychologically speaking. He is a part of OUR family.

Emotions and self-identification can cut both ways. We can also feel guilt or shame for what other people do when we identify with them. For example, during the COVID-19 pandemic, my wife felt personal shame and embarrassment for an email I sent to a parent's group, and we argued about it. I kept thinking, "Why does this bother her so much? The email was my responsibility, not hers." But she identifies with me, and she felt that my behavior reflected poorly on her.

---

[13] Robert C. Roberts, *Emotions in the Moral Life* (Cambridge: Cambridge University Press, 2013).

We do this all the time—we partially identify ourselves with our country, our favorite football teams, and the cars we drive.[14] The fact that we recognize and identify ourselves with things, people, and places outside of us is difficult to explain.[15] As developmental psychologist Philippe Rochat puts it, "What separates me from mine is elusive and forms the major grey area of self-psychology."[16]

Renowned 19th century psychologist William James writes, "[It] is clear that between what a man calls me and what he simply calls mine the line is difficult to draw. We feel and act about certain things that are ours very much as we feel and act about ourselves."[17] He goes on:

> [A] man's Self is the sum total of all that he can call his, not only his body and his psychic powers, but his clothes and his house, his wife and children, his ancestors and friends, his reputation and works, his lands and horses, and yacht and bank-account. All these things give him the same emotions. If they wax and prosper, he feels triumphant; if they dwindle and die away, he feels cast down...

---

[14] Peter Fonagy et al., "Attachment and Personality Pathology," in *The Routledge Handbook of Attachment: Theory*, ed. Paul Holmes and Steve Farnland (New York: Routledge, 2014), 31–48.

[15] Scannell and Gifford, "Defining Place Attachment: A Tripartite Organizing Framework"; Helga Dittmar, *The Social Psychology of Material Possessions: To Have Is to Be* (New York: St. Martin's Press, 1992); Lita Furby, "Understanding the Psychology of Possession and Ownership: A Personal Memoir and an Appraisal of Our Progress," *Journal of Social Behavior and Personality* 6 (1991): 457–63.

[16] See Philippe Rochat, "Possessions and Morality in Early Development," in *Origins of Property Ownership*, New Directions for Child and Adolescent Development 132 (San Francisco: Wiley Periodicals, Inc., 2011), 23–38. The idea that people commonly identify with objects outside the self is generally accepted in psychology. See Pierce, Kostova, and Dirks, "Toward a Theory of Psychological Ownership in Organizations"; Dittmar, *The Social Psychology of Material Possessions: To Have Is to Be*; Douglas J. Porteous, "Home: The Territorial Core," *Geographical Review* 66, no. 4 (1976): 383–90.

[17] William James, *The Principles of Psychology* (New York: Dover, 1890), 291.

When you see something as MINE, you feel as if your "self" is extended to, or recognizable in, that thing.[18] And it is this very "seeing" of something as MINE that is part of what it means to take ownership in our work. The effort we put into our work projects bonds us to them in a special way. We see them as MINE and OURS and want them to succeed because of the same internal drives that make us want to succeed ourselves, more generally. Thus, the capacity to self-identify with something as MINE lies at the heart of psychological ownership.

But what is it, exactly, that are we becoming attached to? It's not just our jobs or roles in an abstract sense. Rather, it's the specific projects and initiatives we pour ourselves into. In the next chapter, we'll explore why projects, not jobs, are the true objects of our psychological ownership—and why this distinction matters for leaders looking to foster an ownership mindset in their teams.

---

[18] F. Cram and H. Paton, "Personal Possessions and Self-Identity: The Experiences of Elderly Women in Three Residential Settings," *Australian Journal of Aging* 12, no. 1 (1993): 19–24; Dittmar, *The Social Psychology of Material Possessions: To Have Is to Be*; Hannah Weisman et al., "Antecedents of Organizational Identification: A Review and Agenda for Future Research," *Journal of Management* 49, no. 6 (2023): 2030–61, https://doi.org/10.1177/01492063221140049.

———————— For Further Reflection ————————

1. Reflect on a time when you felt proud of a team member or your department's accomplishment. How does this experience relate to the concept of self-identification discussed in this chapter?

2. This chapter mentions that self-identification can lead to both positive and negative emotions. How might this insight impact your approach the next time an employee comes to you anxious about something at work?

6

People Own Projects, Not Jobs

"Far and away the best prize that life offers is the chance to work hard at work worth doing."

- Theodore Roosevelt,
the 26th President of the United States

Egyptian Pharaoh Khufu began construction on the Great Pyramid of Giza around 2550 BC. This monumental tomb took more than two decades to build, requiring an estimated 2.3 million stone blocks and the labor of more than 20,000 workers.

Imagine that you are able to go back in time and see the job site. As you walk around, you ask various people how they would define the "project" they are working on. Slaves straining to haul limestone blocks up long ramps tell you they are simply "moving rocks." Artisans carefully chiseling hieroglyphics into the inner chamber walls, however, say they are "telling the great pharaoh's story." When you pose the question to Khufu's vizier, the project manager overseeing the entire endeavor, he proudly declares they are constructing "a gateway to the afterlife" for the pharaoh.

In a sense, all these descriptions are true. The very same construction project can be conceived of and experienced differently. It all depends on one's vantage point. For the laborers straining to move massive stones, it was manual work. For the artisans, it was artistic work recording history. And for the leader, it was sacred work building a tomb to ensure the pharaoh's eternal life.

Figure 6.1 The Great Pyramid of Giza

Much like building a pyramid, an organization can be viewed as a complex set of nested projects. It extends from individual tasks up into task groups, departments, and ultimately, the organizational mission. The organization's overall aim and purpose is the highest level that you can define a "project," but fulfilling this purpose breaks down into the many smaller projects that make it happen. These include projects like developing products, managing operations, and launching marketing campaigns, which can be divided again into all the individual assignments that employees work on together.

In the previous chapter, we discussed the psychological mechanisms of attachment and identification. But we didn't exactly define *what it is* that people become attached to or identify with when they do take ownership *at work*. We're talking about a psychological attachment to "work" instead of people, physical objects, or a place. But what is that, exactly?

Leaders commonly speak about taking ownership in terms of one's "job" or "role."[19] While that may be possible, it misses

---

[19] So do management psychologists. See: He Peng and Jon Pierce, "Job- and Organization-Based Psychological Ownership: Relationship and Outcomes," *Journal of Managerial Psychology* 30, no. 2 (2015): 151–68.

an important point—namely, that a "role" is meaningless apart from how it contributes to a specific *project*. People don't take ownership in roles, themselves. Rather, roles are understood in terms of how they contribute to the aims and goals of projects. So, in reality, people take ownership in projects, not roles. And as we said before, projects can be conceived of at multiple levels.

Figure 6.2

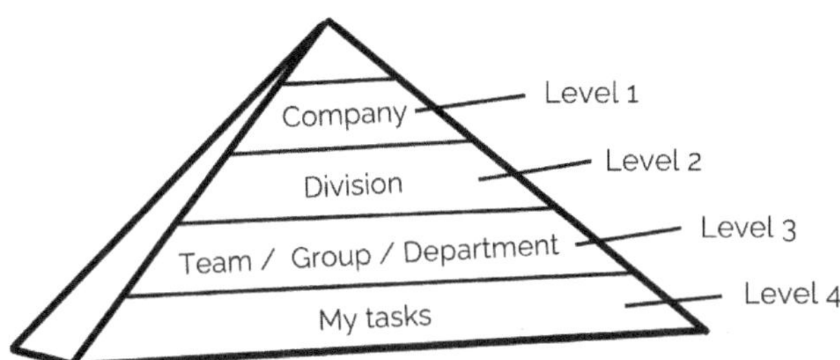

It is most natural for employees to take ownership in the projects, initiatives, and teams that are most immediate to them (see Levels 3 and 4 in the diagram). A person's sense of ownership most naturally expands to the department or division level when they first take on leadership roles (see Levels 2 and 3), because leadership broadens one's perspective, responsibilities, and influence. A sense of ownership at the company-wide level (Level

1) is most naturally developed by founders, executives, or those near the C-suite.[20]

Unless leaders intentionally create a culture where everyone can see their work as contributing to a Level 1 project goal, most people will stay at Levels 3 or 4 in the way they take ownership. Level 1 goals are often too large and abstract for people to "own," unless deliberate efforts have been made to the contrary.

The idea that employees take ownership in projects, not roles, is significant.[21] This often determines how people behave. If employees are only attached to their individual job duties or the projects they work on within small teams, they may perform well in those tasks but lack the drive to solve broader issues. They may also fail to anticipate, or even care about, how their work affects other groups or business units.

In leading for ownership, one of our goals is to have everyone taking ownership at the highest project "level" possible, which is conceptually the organization's primary mission or purpose. Just

---

[20] Organizational identification is a neighboring concept to psychological ownership, and it possibly could be considered a component of psychological ownership. Research in this field has confirmed the possibility of identifying differently with different parts of an organization, but I think understanding attachments to "projects" is a more useful notion. The literature is vast, but for a review of the concepts see Martin R. Edwards, "Organizational Identification: A Conceptual and Operational Review," *International Journal of Management Reviews* 7, no. 4 (2005): 207–30, https://doi.org/10.1111/j.1468-2370.2005.00114.x; Blake E. Ashforth, Spencer H. Harrison, and Kevin G. Corley, "Identification in Organizations: An Examination of Four Fundamental Questions," *Journal of Management* 34, no. 3 (2008): 325–74, https://doi.org/10.1177/0149206308316059; Jeffrey S. Bednar et al., "Putting Identification in Motion: A Dynamic View of Organizational Identification," *Organization Science (Providence, R.I.)* 31, no. 1 (2020): 200–222, https://doi.org/10.1287/orsc.2018.1276; Fred A. Mael and Lois E. Tetrick, "Identifying Organizational Identification. Educational and Psychological Measurement," *Educational and Psychological Measurement* 52, no. 4 (1992): 813–24; Bednar et al., "Putting Identification in Motion."

[21] I argue for this point more extensively in "The Virtue of Taking Ownership" (ProQuest Dissertations Publishing, 2018), https://search.proquest.com/docview/2054314035. Organizational scholars often talk as if people usually take ownership in jobs or organizations.

as Khufu's vizier saw the pyramid as much more than "moving rocks," leaders must empower team members to see how their individual work connects to the greater good. We'll discuss this in much greater detail in the Key of Acceptance section, but for now, just remember that people always take ownership in projects, and within your organization, it's possible to conceive of the same project in different ways.

For Further Reflection

1. Consider the pyramid-building example. How might you help your team members see their work as contributing to a larger, more meaningful project versus performing individual tasks?

2. Think about a recent project in your organization. How might different team members have conceived of this same project at different levels? How could understanding these varying perspectives help you in fostering a stronger sense of ownership across the board?

7

Beliefs That Drive the Ownership Mindset

"The mind is everything. What you think, you become."

- Buddha, spiritual leader and founder of Buddhism

In the bestselling book *Mindset: The New Psychology of Success*, psychologist Carol Dweck introduced the concept of growth and fixed mindsets, illustrating how our beliefs about our abilities and potential can shape our lives.[22] Dweck's work sparked a global conversation about the power of mindset and how it influences our behavior, relationships, and ultimately, our success. But what exactly is a mindset, and how does it relate to our daily lives and taking ownership at work?

A mindset is a set of beliefs and attitudes through which a person experiences their world. It acts as a filter that informs and even changes what we see and how we see it. Most of us have heard of people having an optimistic or a pessimistic mindset. The optimist sees the glass half full, while the pessimist sees the glass half empty. It's the same glass. Only the perspective shifts.

Another example, often cited by success coaches, is the "scarcity versus abundance" mindset. Those with a scarcity

---

[22] Carol S. Dweck, *Mindset: The New Psychology of Success*, Updated edition., Ballantine Books Trade Paperback edition. (New York: Ballantine Books, 2016).

mindset believe that resources and opportunities are limited, leading to a fear-based approach to life. In contrast, individuals with an abundance mindset trust there are ample resources and possibilities, which fosters a more open and generous outlook. The ownership mindset is similar: it shapes the way we see and interpret our experiences at work.

A shift from one mindset to another can change how we behave and interact with the world because mindsets change how we interpret both new information and the behaviors of others.[23] They affect the way we *feel* about situations and may significantly change our moods and attitudes.

> "Mindsets are often formed unintentionally as the product of external environmental factors and past experiences."

Mindsets can also be cultivated. For example, people can develop mindsets of gratitude and thankfulness through practice. Research shows that positive mindsets like these actually increase a person's happiness and life satisfaction.[24] People can likewise develop negative mindsets. For example, learned helplessness and

---

[23] For example, when romantic partners have optimistic attitudes toward each other, that positive idealization both *buffers* and *transforms* the way behavior and new information is interpreted. See: Sandra L. Murray, John G. Holmes, and Dale W. Griffin, "The Benefits of Positive Illusions: Idealization and the Construction of Satisfaction in Close Relationships," *Journal of Personality and Social Psychology* 70, no. 1 (1996): 79–98, https://doi.org/10.1037/0022-3514.70.1.79; Sandra L. Murray, John G. Holmes, and Dale W. Griffin, "The Self-Fulfilling Nature of Positive Illusions in Romantic Relationships: Love Is Not Blind, but Prescient," *Journal of Personality and Social Psychology* 71, no. 6 (1996): 1155–80, https://doi.org/10.1037/0022-3514.71.6.1155.

[24] Wenceslao Unanue et al., "The Reciprocal Relationship Between Gratitude and Life Satisfaction: Evidence From Two Longitudinal Field Studies," *Frontiers in Psychology* 10 (2019): 2480–2480, https://doi.org/10.3389/fpsyg.2019.02480.

the victim mindset decrease happiness and are associated with depression, anxiety,[25] and decreased performance.[26]

Mindsets are often formed unintentionally as the product of external environmental factors and past experiences. This is important to recognize. I have spoken to many executives and business owners who complain that people at their companies don't have an ownership mindset. But they often fail to see how their company's culture, structure, and past management practices actually *stifled* their employees' abilities to take on the ownership mindset.

People can intentionally choose to change and develop new mindsets[27] with some effort. In that way, mindsets are like other habits. Just like going to the gym can become a habit, mindsets can become habits of perception and thought. And once they become habitual, they are embedded into our experience. They shape what we notice, or fail to notice, in the world around us.

Consider grateful people. They have trained themselves to "look" for positive things and give thanks, and are happier as a result. An ungrateful person focuses on what they do not have and what they want, and are less satisfied as a result. Grateful and ungrateful people can experience *the very same situations* and feel totally different about them. They just approach the situation with a different interpretive lens, or mindset.

---

[25] Christopher Peterson, *Learned Helplessness: A Theory for the Age of Personal Control* (New York: Oxford University Press, 1993).

[26] Mark J. Martinko and William L. Gardner, "Learned Helplessness: An Alternative Explanation for Performance Deficits," *The Academy of Management Review* 7, no. 2 (1982): 195–204, https://doi.org/10.5465/amr.1982.4285559.

[27] David S. Yeager et al., "A National Experiment Reveals Where a Growth Mindset Improves Achievement," *Nature* 573, no. 7774 (2019): 364–69, https://doi.org/10.1038/s41586-019-1466-y.

Before reading any further, take a look at this illustration and ask yourself what you see:

Figure 7.1

This figure is known as the duck-rabbit, because it is possible to see the drawing as either a duck or as a rabbit. When most people first look at the image, they only see one animal. It is usually only *after* they are prompted to look for something else that they see the other animal.

I showed this drawing as a part of a presentation to a 12-person management team at a leadership retreat. Most people could see both drawings, but there were three people in the room who could see only the duck. Just telling them to look for both the duck and the rabbit wasn't enough. I had to physically point to parts of the drawing for them to see both animals. I showed them how the ears of the rabbit can also be seen as the duck's bill, and how the eye can be seen as looking in one direction or another.

This is an important point for leaders to understand. Often people must be shown *how* to take a different perspective. Once we have adopted a particular mindset, we may require someone else to help us see things differently. It's no different with the ownership mindset.

When employees start to practice and operate with an ownership mindset, it will change how they see their work and their impact and contribution as a part of your company. One of your jobs as a leader is to help them make that shift in perception.

Let's quickly review our model of psychological ownership.

Figure 4.1

THE PSYCHOLOGY OF OWNERSHIP

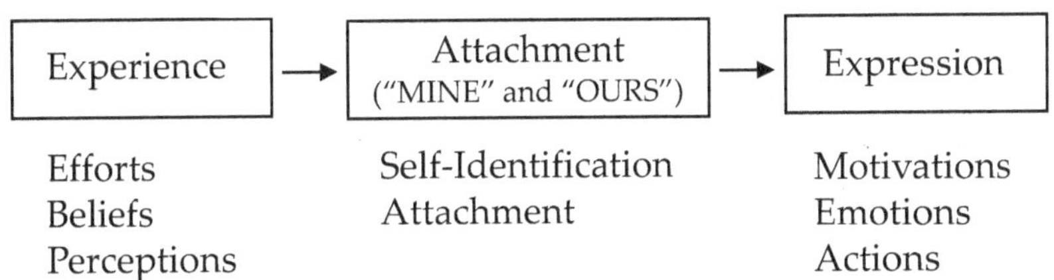

The box on the left represents the experiences we have at work. Part of our experience involves the time and effort we invest. The other part of our experience includes what we believe about our work and how we perceive the results of our time and effort. This forms a feedback loop. The loop is key to understanding why people who take ownership in their work often continue to do so, and why those who lack a sense of ownership often seem stuck there. Our beliefs inform our perceptions, and our perceptions inform the beliefs we have about our reality. Eventually, this combination of beliefs and perceptions form a mindset. And our mindset is critical in determining whether or not we become attached to our work.

PUTTING IT TOGETHER

Let's now clarify all these concepts by looking at a real-life example (fictionalized for anonymity). Susan is an administrative assistant at a tool manufacturing company. When she first took the job, Susan was eager to do her best and engaged enthusiastically with her work. She took initiative to streamline administrative processes and volunteered to plan company events. Susan believed that her efforts contributed to the company's success and that her role kept things running smoothly.

However, Susan sensed over time that no one noticed all her hard work. Her manager rarely provided feedback and dismissed many of her process improvement ideas. For one product launch, Susan stayed late every night. She later overheard the executives thanking the sales team for working tirelessly, but no one said anything to her.

Susan began to perceive that her extra efforts didn't matter. She formed the belief that management didn't even want her to take initiative anymore. She stopped volunteering for extra projects and declined the company's invitation to serve on a diversity committee, something she normally would have been eager to do. As a single mother with two kids, Susan needed her job—so, although she remained punctual and responsible for the tasks she was assigned, Susan started doing only what was asked. Nothing more. Her motivation, emotional investment, and sense of ownership dried up.

As Susan's story illustrates, work experiences can significantly reshape our mindsets. Susan's mindset shifted from being one of ownership (seeing her work as MINE) to one that was responsible but detached.

The good news is that most employees naturally want to take ownership in their work if you can help them shift their mindset. That's because taking ownership within work projects is connected to each person's psychological need to express agency and exert influence over their world.[28] The bad news is that ownership attachments can be "killed" when the mindset is not supported.

So, what exactly are the beliefs and perceptions of someone who possesses an ownership mindset?

Table 1 contains some—and only some—of the beliefs someone with an ownership mindset holds, along with the perceptions that regularly support and reinforce those beliefs.

Table 7.1 – Beliefs and Perceptions of the Ownership Mindset

Belief	Associated Perception
My boss / this company wants me to take ownership at work.	I see that problem solving and new ideas are welcomed and invited.
My work contributes to something good and worthwhile.	I see how my company's products and services make the world a better place.
My efforts make a difference here. My ideas are acted upon. I share in the company's success.	I easily perceive how my efforts contribute to our mutual success and change outcomes.
I have a good future here.	I see how I can grow and continue my career with this company.

These beliefs and associated perceptions correspond to the Four Keys we'll discuss in the rest of the book. For now, it's important to understand that a person naturally identifies with and becomes more attached to their work (i.e., takes ownership) when these belief/perception pairings are supported.

---

28 Furby, "Understanding the Psychology of Possession and Ownership: A Personal Memoir and an Appraisal of Our Progress"; Dittmar, *The Social Psychology of Material Possessions: To Have Is to Be*; Graham Brown, Jon L. Pierce, and Craig Crossley, "Toward an Understanding of the Development of Ownership Feelings," *Journal of Organizational Behavior* 35 (2014): 318–38.

When an ownership mindset is in place, people are more likely to filter new experiences through their beliefs and prior perceptions. Even when they occasionally have an experience that does not support ownership, it is likely to be interpreted as an exception and not cause someone to detach from their work.

Contrast that with the beliefs and associated perceptions of someone who lacks a sense of ownership in their work, found in Table 2.

**Table 7.2 – Beliefs and Perceptions of Someone
Lacking a Sense of Ownership**

Belief	Associated Perception
My boss wants me to do just what I'm told and no more.	I perceive problem solving and initiative are not welcomed.
My work contributes only to the company making money.	I fail to see how my company's products and services make the world a better place.
My ideas are usually ignored. My best efforts rarely change anything. My work doesn't matter much to the company's success.	I fail to see how my work matters in the grand scheme of things.
I've hit the ceiling and have no future here. I don't belong here.	I perceive that I won't be able to advance my career, pay, or responsibilities here. These are not my people.

When a person holds these beliefs and associated perceptions, how could it ever be possible for them to take ownership of their work? It's not. In fact, if a person holds just even one of these anti-ownership beliefs or routinely perceives their work in one of these ways, it's likely that they will become detached—if they aren't already. This is exactly why there is an employee engagement crisis, as represented by the Gallup statistics cited earlier.

A person's beliefs and perceptions about their work either give rise to a natural identification with and attachment to work, or they do not. The attachment must come from within. As a leader, you need to recognize that cultivating a sense of ownership in someone is something that can only be done through shifts in perception. It cannot be coerced.

Once a person acquires an ownership mindset, however, things become easier. In many ways, it's like a relationship. In marriage, one can build up a sense of trust and positive beliefs about their relationship with a spouse. When this mindset is present, it helps one to interpret small actions in ways that don't damage the overall relationship. For example, if my spouse is rude or says something that hurts my feelings in some way, it does not have to jeopardize our relationship. I can interpret such actions as her having a bad day. But not all marriages are like this. Some spouses can have a very negative mindset about their relationship. This can cause even small and unintentional offenses to seem big, and the distrust between partners can turn molehills into mountains.

The core beliefs and ways of seeing the world that constitute our mindsets are much like habits. They aren't created in a day, nor are they lost overnight. It takes time for us to truly inhabit them. Using the Keys in this book to unlock a sense of ownership must become an essential and habitual part of your leadership practice if you want to change the mindsets of those you lead.

Next, we'll explore how the ownership mindset shapes the behaviors, motivations, and emotions of your team.

———————————— For Further Reflection ————————————

1. Consider the beliefs and associated perceptions listed in Table 1 (Ownership Mindset) and Table 2 (Lacking Ownership). Which ones are most prevalent on your team(s)? How might you reinforce positive beliefs and address negative ones?

2. The chapter mentions that mindsets can be cultivated intentionally. As a leader, what specific actions could you take to help foster an ownership mindset among your team members?

3. The duck-rabbit illustration demonstrates how people might need help seeing things from a different perspective. In your leadership role, how can you better guide your team members to "see" their work and contributions from an ownership perspective?

8

How Ownership Transforms Motivation, Emotion, and Behavior

"Emotions are not good or bad - it's how we respond to them that matters."

- MARC BRACKETT, founding director of the
Yale Center for Emotional Intelligence

Imagine two software developers, Alex and Jamie, working on the same project. Both are talented, but their approaches couldn't be more different.

Alex arrives at 9 AM sharp, meticulously follows the project specifications, and leaves promptly at 5 PM. When faced with a bug, Alex dutifully logs it and moves on to the next task. The project is just another job to Alex.

Jamie, on the other hand, loses track of time while coding. When Jamie encounters a bug, it becomes a personal challenge. Jamie stays late, consults with colleagues, and won't rest until a solution is found. For Jamie, this project isn't just work—it's a creation, a reflection of personal skill and dedication.

What's the difference between Alex and Jamie? It's not talent or training—it's ownership.

The transformation that ownership creates in our work lives is profound, yet often misunderstood. It's easy to spot the symptoms of ownership—increased productivity, emotional investment, proactive behavior—but understanding the underlying psychology is crucial for any leader hoping to foster this mindset in their team.

In this chapter we'll break down how the ownership attachment transforms our work lives through its three key expressions: motivation, emotion, and behavior.

Figure 4.1

THE PSYCHOLOGY OF OWNERSHIP

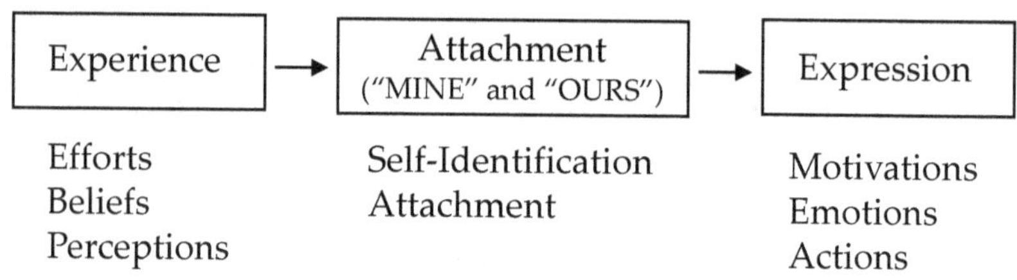

MOTIVATION: FROM MY PAYCHECK TO MY PURPOSE

The motivational shift that comes with ownership is akin to the difference between renting and owning a home. Renters might keep the place tidy, but owners renovate, landscape, and constantly think about improvements.

In my years as a leader, I witnessed this transformation firsthand. Team members who took ownership stopped asking, "What do you want me to do?" and started saying, "Here's what I think we should do." Their source of motivation shifted from external (pleasing the boss, or earning a paycheck) to internal (pride in the work, or desire for project success).

But there's a psychological nuance here that we must not overlook. When we take ownership, our motivation also becomes partially self-reflexive. Yes, we want our projects to succeed because of the good they do in the world or the value they bring to the company. But we also want them to succeed simply because they're OURS.

When I take ownership of a project, I take special care of it because I want it to succeed—not just because I view it as good or expect a payoff, but also because it is MINE. It's what *I* am working on with my time, energy, and effort. Yes, I must see the project as worthwhile, or I won't identify with it in the first place. But the self-reflexive aspect of an owner's motivation creates a powerful drive that goes beyond external rewards or even the project's inherent value.

EMOTION: FROM INDIFFERENCE TO INVESTMENT

Ownership also transforms our emotional relationship with work. It's the difference between watching a sports game as a casual observer versus watching your child play—suddenly, every move matters intensely.

I experienced this contrast firsthand in my role as a product manager. I always had a *project manager* on my team who was responsible for maintaining the project plan, creating and updating the project schedule, and providing forecasts based on how things tracked. I'll never forget one particular project manager, Steve. I felt very puzzled working with him. Whenever our team was in danger of missing a milestone or deadline, or whenever our project experienced delays or setbacks, or we got other bad news, he seemed completely unfazed—not in the least bit worried or upset.

On the other hand, I would fret and go into problem-solving mode. I called meetings, looked for workarounds, and did everything in my power to get things back on track. I never knew how to interpret these differences in temperament, and I often wondered if there was something wrong with me. I suspected that he must have a greater degree of emotional intelligence. I grew up in the era where people often said, "It's just business, not personal," but I always seemed to take things personally.

Initially, I thought Steve's calm demeanor indicated superior emotional intelligence. But I came to realize that my emotional investment—my distress over setbacks and joy in successes[29]—was a natural consequence of how I took ownership. I cared because the project was MINE. To Steve, the obstacles to our success were not "his" problem. He took no ownership of them. His job was to enter updates into the software, and that's precisely what he did. Nothing more.

This emotional connection can be a double-edged sword, of course. While it drives commitment and excellence, it can also lead to stress and burnout if not properly managed. The key is finding the right balance—caring deeply without over-identifying.

ACTION: FROM REACTIVE TO PROACTIVE

Perhaps the most visible transformation that ownership creates is in behavior, which, of course, flows directly from our motivations and emotions. Non-owners wait for instructions; owners anticipate needs and take initiative. Owners have a *proactive stance* toward their projects. That stance often involves proactive problem solving, as well as proactively creating or improving a company's processes, products or services. By proactive, I simply mean that somebody else didn't ask them to do it. Owners naturally think of ways to grow revenue, serve more customers, and become more efficient on their own.

In tech startups, this behavioral shift is often the difference between success and failure. I've known developers who own their projects working through weekends to meet launch deadlines, not

---

[29] Robert C. Roberts, *Emotions: An Essay in Aid of Moral Psychology* (Cambridge; New York: Cambridge University Press, 2003).

because anyone asked them to, but because they couldn't bear to see their creation delayed.

Or take the case of Paul, a line worker at a car manufacturing plant. Unlike his colleagues who simply reported defects, Paul took it upon himself to analyze the root causes of recurring issues. His proactive approach led to changes in the production process that significantly reduced defect rates.

THE TRANSFORMATIVE POWER OF OWNERSHIP

That concludes our deep dive into ownership psychology. The model of psychological ownership I've presented here is the driving force for the rest of the book. It serves as the basis for all Four Keys and informs the leadership strategies and habits that I hope you will adopt.

Understanding how ownership transforms us is more than an academic exercise. It provides crucial insights into how we can create work environments where people feel genuinely invested in their projects and the success of our organizations. When individuals develop a sense of ownership, they tend to bring more of themselves to their work—their creativity, their problem-solving skills, and their unique perspectives.

You can now understand why psychological ownership cannot be imposed—it must be organically cultivated by (re) shaping people's experiences and work culture. As leaders, our role is to create conditions where ownership can flourish, rather than trying to force it into existence.

As we move forward, we'll explore many leadership practices that foster the ownership mindset, organized around the Four Keys. These practices are grounded in the psychological principles we've discussed, aiming to shape experiences, beliefs, and perceptions that allow people to genuinely attach to their work.

The journey to creating a culture of ownership is complex and multifaceted. It requires patience, trust, and a willingness to reconsider traditional management approaches. However, the potential benefits—including increased retention, innovation, and job satisfaction—make it a worthwhile endeavor for any organization.

In the sections that follow, we'll delve into each of the Four Keys so that you can unlock this transformative process within your teams. By understanding and applying these keys, you'll be better equipped to create an environment where ownership can take root and thrive.

For Further Reflection

1. Think about a time when you felt strong ownership over a project. How did this affect your motivation, emotions, and actions? How can you use this personal experience to better understand and cultivate ownership in your team members?

2. Reflect on a recent project in your organization. How did team members express ownership (or lack thereof) through their motivations, emotions, and actions? What insights does this give you about their level of psychological ownership?

3. Consider the concept of proactive behavior as an expression of ownership. How can you create an environment that encourages and rewards proactive problem solving and innovation in your team?

4. The chapter emphasizes that psychological ownership cannot be imposed but must be organically cultivated. What specific changes in your leadership approach or organizational culture might help create the right conditions for ownership to take root?

Section Summary

Decoding Ownership Psychology

- Understanding the psychology of ownership is crucial for leaders aiming to create a culture where employees naturally and willingly take ownership of their work and the organization's mission.

- Psychological ownership is a form of human attachment to work, emerging as we invest effort and identify with projects as MINE or OURS. This attachment is at the core of the ownership mindset.

- Ownership psychology involves both self-identification with work and attachment to it. This cannot be imposed. It must be organically cultivated by shaping supportive work experiences, clarifying purpose, and fostering an environment where employees feel valued and influential.

- People take ownership in projects, not roles or jobs. Organizations are nested hierarchies of projects, and individuals can take ownership at various levels—depending on their perspective—from specific tasks to the company's overall mission. Part of a leader's job is to elevate employees' conceptions of their projects to Level 1.

- Mindsets—as filtering beliefs and perceptions—shape our work experiences and can support or hinder ownership. The "ownership mindset" is not innate but can be cultivated through intentional leadership practices.

- Expressions of psychological ownership include: intrinsic motivation to care for one's projects, emotional investment in outcomes, and proactive, self-initiated behavior that ensures project success.

KEY #1
THE INVITATION

9

Key Concept:
You Must Invite Others
to Take Ownership

"Something happens when you feel ownership. You no longer act like a spectator or consumer, because you're an owner."

— Bob Goff, former attorney and
bestselling author of *Love Does*

Aconstruction industry client had some rather serious performance issues with a foreman who wouldn't engage in his work. He frequently dropped the ball on tasks, which caused bottlenecks and missed deadlines on multiple building projects. Customers were getting upset.

The company's founder and a senior HR leader called a meeting to talk to him about his performance. They decided to focus the conversation on ownership, emphasizing how much they wanted him to *own* each facet of the various projects he managed. When the foreman pushed back in the meeting, putting blame on external factors, they reiterated their message: *we really want YOU to own your work. Completely.*

Very quickly afterward, the company saw a shift in this employee's attitude and how he approached his work. Four months later, he seemed like a different person. He went from being a problem employee to one of the company all-stars. Supplies were ordered when they needed to be ordered. Steps were no longer missed. His projects finished on time and under budget.

The CEO later pointed to their conversation about ownership as the key turning point. Certainly, other conversations and course corrections occurred along the way, but that first talk was the catalyst. Needless to say, this leadership team has now made it a practice to speak to all their employees about taking ownership of their work.

Inviting your employees to take ownership is one of the simplest and yet most overlooked ways to start creating a culture of ownership within your teams. It's really that simple. You offer it to them. You explain to an individual what taking ownership really means, and then you describe what it would look like in their role. You tell them clearly and directly that your *desire* is that they start taking ownership.

People studying the psychology of ownership have discovered that ownership is a socially constructed reality.[30] If you were the only person living on an island, the concept of ownership would

---

[30] Both Rousseau and Hume argue that the nature of property is essentially social. See Jean-Jacques Rousseau, *Discourse on Inequality* (New York: Penguin Books, 1984). See David Hume, *Essays, Moral, Political and Literary; An Enquiry Concerning the Principles of Morals*, ed. T.H. Green and T.H. Grosse (London: Longmans, Green, and Co., 1898), 179–82. Economist Harold Demsetz offers a similar contemporary perspective on ownership. Harold Demsetz, "Toward a Theory of Property Rights," *American Economic Review* 62 (1967): 347–59. An object's social history also seems to play an important role in ownership; see: Ori Friedman et al., "Ownership and Object History," in *Origins of Property Ownership*, New Directions for Child and Adolescent Development 132 (San Francisco: Wiley Periodicals, Inc., 2011), 79–89. See also: James K. Beggan, "On the Social Nature of Nonsocial Perception: The Mere Ownership Effect," *Journal of Personality and Social Psychology* 62, no. 2 (1992): 229–37; Charles Kalish and Craig D. Anderson, "Ownership as a Social Status," in *Origins of Property Ownership*, New Directions for Child and Adolescent Development 132 (San Francisco: Wiley Periodicals, Inc., 2011), 65–77.

not mean anything. In the context of work projects, people take on the ownership of tasks, activities, roles, outputs, and so forth in part because these things are communicated to them as being *theirs*.

The idea that ownership is a socially constructed reality isn't just a theoretical point. It's of practical importance because employees don't always know when or if they should take ownership in their projects.

Almost every new employee, from a factory worker to a senior executive, starts out in their new position without a full sense of ownership.[31] They ask themselves questions like:

"What am I supposed to do here?"

"What is expected of me?"

"What are my daily and monthly responsibilities?"

These are the pressing questions for any new employee. Leaders easily overlook this fact because they've been in their businesses for so long. But you must remember that people don't start in your organization able to fully take ownership, because initially they are just trying to figure things out. Most people come into organizations with an employee mindset, and that is okay. It's the job of leaders in an organization to transition new hires from thinking only as an employee to adopting the mindset of an owner. The goal is to do this quickly.

> "Employees must often be 'given' ownership, so to speak. That means the first step in offering ownership is communication."

It all starts with communication. Employees must often be "given" ownership, so to speak. That means the first step in

---

[31] Perhaps an exception to this is a founding entrepreneur who is just starting a company. But for anyone who is joining an organization that is already up and running, this will be true.

offering ownership is communication. You must communicate your desire and expectation that each person will take ownership as soon as they feel comfortable. You also need to explain what taking ownership means by giving them some practical examples. Describe how someone taking ownership in that specific role or context might act. If you as a leader don't know what taking ownership looks like in that role, how can you expect them to?

Invitations to ownership can happen in one-on-one conversations and team meetings. A broad invitation to ownership can also be instilled in an organization's culture by adopting ownership as a core value. This is what companies like InfoTrust have done.[32] Ownership is one of their company core values. In an ideal world, invitations to ownership would be made at all three levels—to individuals, teams, and company-wide.

These invitations to ownership must also be made *regularly*. In other words, they need to become habitual for you as a leader. The appeal to take ownership must be consistently reiterated and reinforced. One of the best ways to reinforce your invitation to ownership is to praise people when they demonstrate a sense of ownership through their actions.

It's natural for conversations about ownership to progress over time. For example, after some initial conversations, you might later discuss how it's possible to take too much ownership in one's work. Even though you want your people to be invested, you don't want extreme ownership to lead to burnout or fatigue. In fact, studies have shown that it's actually important for people

---

[32] Lisa Wilms, "What Ownership in the Workplace Means to Me," *InfoTrust* (blog), March 24, 2017, https://infotrust.com/articles/what-ownership-in-the-workplace-means-to-me/.

to detach from their work in non-work hours.[33] Likewise, your "invitation" discussions might touch on the importance of projects being owned in common—in other words, it's best for people to see projects as OURS and not merely as "MINE." (See Section 5 for more on this.)

In the chapters that follow, we'll look at five different leadership practices that can help you invite your employees to ownership as you manage them day to day.

———————————— For Further Reflection ————————————

1. Think about a recent project or task you assigned to a team member. How explicitly did you invite them to take ownership? How might the outcome have differed if you had made this invitation clearer?

2. Consider your onboarding process for new employees. How and when do you introduce the concept of ownership? What specific steps could you take to make this introduction more effective?

3. Reflect on a time when you noticed an employee demonstrating ownership. How did you respond? How could you make praising and reinforcing ownership behaviors a more regular part of your leadership practice?

---

[33] Sabine Sonnentag and Caterina Schiffner, "Psychological Detachment from Work during Nonwork Time and Employee Well-Being: The Role of Leader's Detachment," *The Spanish Journal of Psychology* 22 (2019): E3–E3, https://doi.org/10.1017/sjp.2019.2; Justin Oakley and Dean Cocking, "Professional Detachment in Healthcare and Legal Practice," in *Virtue Ethics and Professional Roles* (Cambridge: Cambridge University Press, 2001); Sabine Sonnentag, Carmen Binnewies, and Eva J. Mojza, "Staying Well and Engaged When Demands Are High: The Role of Psychological Detachment," *Journal of Applied Psychology* 95, no. 5 (2010): 965–76, https://doi.org/10.1037/a0020032.

10

How to Ignite Ownership in One-on-Ones

"Ownership is a mindset, not a job description. It's about taking responsibility for the outcomes of your work, regardless of your role or title."

- Liz Wiseman, author of *Multipliers: How the Best Leaders Make Everyone Smarter*

The most powerful "invitation" to ownership that you can give someone is during a one-on-one conversation. This conversation doesn't have to be long—five to 10 minutes can suffice. But it's a critical conversation to have, and it's one that should be revisited regularly.

The agenda is simple: You are going to clearly and directly explain to an employee that you want them to take ownership of their work. Of course, there are more or less artful ways of doing this. What follows is a model conversation between Sarah, a printing company team leader, and Tom, a new line worker who operates a large printing press. Notice how she offers ownership to Tom. After the dialogue, we'll outline the structure of this conversation so you can implement it in your own context. Tom has been on the job for two months.

SARAH: Hi Tom. How are things going with the printing press? I noticed you haven't had to ask me many questions recently.

TOM: Yeah, I am getting the hang of it. I feel comfortable running the offset jobs, but I'm still having trouble with some of the more difficult bleed setups.

SARAH: That's great. Those machines can be complicated, but I think you're adapting really well.

TOM: Thanks.

SARAH: I wanted to speak to you a little more about your continued development at the company.

TOM: Oh, okay. What do you mean?

SARAH: Well, when a new person starts on my team, I like to give them a month or so to learn their jobs and get settled in. But then I like to have a conversation about ownership—specifically, how you can start taking ownership in your work. Although we train each person to do their job as best as we know how, that training is usually based on how the previous person did it, or how we've always done things.

But that isn't always the best way to work, nor is it necessarily the best way to serve our customers. I'm a firm believer that there is always room for improvement. I also want the team to feel freedom to personalize how they get their work done, while staying within the broad process boundaries we have in place.

All that's to say, I'd love to see you start taking ownership of your work. Your role on our team is so important, and you are a critical part of this company. As you see better ways to do things, or ways that we might improve, I want you to feel empowered to make changes.

If you think a change might affect another team member or our overall process, we should have a conversation about it first—but other things you could just change without asking, as long as you feel confident it will make things better. For example: the way you perform specific tasks, the order in which you do things, how you run the machinery, or where and how you store supplies. There are many possibilities. The fact is, you are closer to your own work than I am. You know your job better than me or anyone else.

TOM: Wow. Okay, I think I understand.

SARAH: If you ever think there are improvements we can make as a team, or even as a company, I want to hear about them. That's part of what it means for us all to take ownership together. My role is to empower people to serve our customers well. Of course, not every new idea can be implemented. But if we at least discuss them and do what we can, this place will be a much better place to work, and we'll stay ahead of our competition. Does that make sense?

TOM: Yes, I think so.

SARAH: Great. I encourage you to start thinking about our print production process as an owner would—like it's your baby. Even if your job responsibilities are limited to one part of the process, I want you to start thinking about the whole. Whenever there are delays, hiccups, breakdowns, supply shortages—really, whatever problems you may see or encounter—I want you to think about solving them like an owner would. On this team, we are all co-owners. A delay or issue is *our* problem, not someone else's. It's both your problem and our problem until we get it solved.

I'm always here to support you, of course. But the point is that I want to encourage you to start taking ownership of things on your own. If you can solve it on your own, do it.

TOM: Okay, I get that.

SARAH: I've worked with two types of people: People who point the finger and make excuses when things go bad, and people who take ownership to get things fixed no matter where or why the problem started. I want you to be that second kind of person.

Do you understand what I'm asking?

TOM: Totally. At my last job, every problem was someone else's problem. People were always pointing fingers. I have to confess I've done this myself a few times.

SARAH: Right. I've fallen into that same trap. But this is an invitation for you to start thinking like an owner. I want everyone on this team to think as an owner would, me included, so that we can all be good stewards of our company's mission.

TOM: I understand.

SARAH: Great. That's all I have for now. I'm really excited you are here, and I don't want this to be just another job where you feel like all you can do is take orders. I want you to know that I value you, and that your work matters. In whatever ways you can take ownership, I want you to know officially that I support that.

TOM: Thanks, Sarah.

SARAH: And don't worry, this won't be the only conversation we'll have about this. In our next meeting, I want to talk to you more about how our team serves the other departments in the company and the importance of what we do. I want to make sure you really understand how our products serve our customers and make people's lives better. It can be easy to lose sight of that in the day-to-day running of our presses. But one thing at a time. Any questions for me right now?

TOM: Nope. That sounds good. I appreciate that and will do my best to start thinking like an owner. Thank you!

This dialogue serves as model for what a good "invitation" to take ownership can look like. Invitations like this are almost guaranteed to ignite an employee's sense of ownership. In the conversation, you can see Sarah employing good leadership habits, such as approaching the conversation with empathy, appreciation, and curiosity, in addition to her main offer of ownership.

Let's break it down into four easy steps:

1. *Acknowledge a person's progress and strengths.* Sarah begins by highlighting Tom's progress and growing competence in his role, making him feel valued and appreciated. Sarah wants Tom to be open and receptive to receive her invitation to ownership as something positive, not something constructive or critical. This sets the stage for what comes next.

2. *Introduce the concept of ownership.* Sarah explains what she means by "ownership," specifically in regard to Tom's work. She emphasizes the importance of taking initiative and defines ownership in the context of continuous improvement, describing it as both proactive and problem-solving. Sarah encourages Tom to identify better ways of doing things because there's always room for improvement, and she explicitly empowers him to make changes that will improve his work. Finally, she encourages him to think like an owner by taking ownership and finding solutions for *any* problem he finds, rather than simply pointing fingers or making excuses.

3. *Invite collaboration and offer support.* Sarah offers support while encouraging independence. She assures Tom that she's available to help him when needed, but she likewise

invites him to take ownership and to solve problems on his own whenever possible. This balance of support and autonomy is essential for fostering a sense of ownership and continuous growth. She also encourages Steve to discuss any ideas that would positively affect the team or improve their overall process. She emphasizes the "we" of ownership, which promotes a sense of collaboration.

4. *Commit to continued dialogue.* Sarah sets the expectation for future conversations, ensuring ongoing communication and support for Steve's growth in how he takes ownership. She previews that she wants to explain the team's work in the context of serving others at the company and the big picture "good" that the company delivers to the marketplace. We'll learn more about the importance of this in the next section when we talk about the Key of Acceptance. But for now, Steve is left knowing that he can approach Sarah freely if he still has questions.

To conclude, intentionally inviting your employees to ownership in a one-on-one conversation is a crucial step toward unlocking the ownership mindset. The key to making this conversation successful, of course, is that you have to mean it. You can't invite people to ownership and then micromanage them or consistently shut down their ideas. In other words, you'll also need to commit to the other leadership practices described in this book.

Inviting ownership in one-on-one conversations will make your people feel valued and empowered. This makes them more likely to go above and beyond, drive innovation, and contribute to your team's long-term success.

Now is the time to act. You don't even have to finish reading this book. Start scheduling one-on-one ownership conversations with those you lead today. Then make it a habit to revisit your invitations to ownership often, both with new and existing team members.

---------------------------- Take Action ----------------------------

Offer Ownership in One-on-Ones

1. **Schedule one-on-one meetings**. In the next week, set up individual meetings with at least three team members. These could be your direct reports or key individuals you want to empower.

2. **Prepare your talking points**. Before each meeting, jot down specific notes on:

   o The individual's recent progress or strengths.

   o How their role contributes to the team or company's success.

   o Areas where you'd like to see them take more ownership.

   o Examples of what ownership looks like in their specific role.

3. **Conduct the ownership conversation**. During each meeting, follow the four-step structure outlined in the chapter:

   o Acknowledge their progress and strengths.

   o Introduce the concept of ownership.

   o Invite collaboration and offer support.

   o Commit to continued dialogue.

4. **Follow up**. After each meeting, send a brief email summarizing the key points of your conversation about ownership. Include any specific actions or changes that result from this conversation.

5. **Set a reminder**. Schedule a follow-up conversation with each team member in four to six weeks to discuss how they're taking ownership in their work and address any challenges they've encountered.

11

Why Questions Are More Powerful Than Answers

"Coaching isn't an addition to a leader's job, it's an integral part of it."

- GEORGE S. ODIORNE, author of
Management by Objectives

Imagine the following scenario: one of your team members just ran into an issue, and now they're stuck. You have encountered the same issue before and know just how to fix it. They ask you for a solution.

What do you do?

Most of us are tempted to go ahead and solve the problem. We tell our employees what to do and then move on. In doing so, we have good intentions. Solving someone else's problem alleviates their pain and speeds up the process. We pat ourselves on the back. Our hard-won expertise has helped someone else. Everybody wins...right?

Well, not exactly.

Have you ever considered that your habit of solving problems for other people might be one of your greatest weaknesses as a leader? Many leaders unconsciously stifle their employees'

> "Every time one of your employees comes to you with a problem, look at it as an opportunity to *invite them to take ownership.*"

development and sense of ownership by providing them answers instead of coaching them to solve problems on their own.

In fact, one of the most difficult judgment calls that good leaders face daily is how much to help people versus letting them struggle to find their own solutions. It's like being a parent. If you always tie your children's shoes, they never learn to do it on their own. Worse, they learn to be dependent on you and won't *want* to do it on their own. I actually made this mistake with my three-year-old son, and it took a lot of work to undo. "No, Daddy, you do it," is what I heard for what seemed like ages.

Here is a reframe that you need to make if you want to lead for ownership: every time one of your employees comes to you with a problem, look at it as an opportunity to *invite them to take ownership*. When you give an answer or tell them immediately what to do, you take that opportunity away. That person then merely executes your instructions, which actually means that *you* took ownership of the problem, not them. The result is a lost opportunity for them to think and act like an owner. Once you learn to stop fixing your team members' problems, they will be forced to solve them on their own. That is what owners do—owners solve problems and don't leave things to someone else.

In your role as a *leader*, of course, you want to be a supportive resource for your people. You don't want to undermine the sense of collaboration and mutual support. You've got to be there for those you lead, but you can do this without solving all their problems or dispensing wisdom from your wealth of experience like a candy machine. Instead, help your employees take ownership by asking them questions when they come to you with problems. Stop giving answers.

In his book *The Coaching Habit*, Michael Bungay Stanier, an executive coach and the founder of MBS.works and Box of Crayons, suggests a series of three powerful questions that you can ask employees who face roadblocks.[34] Remember, *every* problem they face is an opportunity for you to invite them to ownership.

The first question he calls the focus question. It is designed to help people get to the heart of an issue. After listening to them initially describe the problem, you ask:

QUESTION 1: "What's the real challenge for you here?"

The key is to get them to explain the real challenge for *them*, not the issue generally, or what the problem is for "everybody." Then, no matter how they answer, probe further:

"And what else?" (Or "What else is the real challenge for you here?")

There is almost always more that needs to come out after the first attempt. So much so, that it's usually worth saying a third time, "And what else?"

Now that you've given them a chance to clarify the issues, you ask them the second question:

QUESTION 2: "What do you want (to happen)?"

This question is powerful because it puts ownership in their hands. This person came to you for answers. They came to find out what *you* wanted them to do about the problem. And unless they had a possible solution in mind, they likely already felt divorced from ownership. But you're going to turn the tables. By asking them what *they* want out of the situation, you help them start to answer the problem on their own.

Next, after you've helped them (1) clarify the real issues and (2) ask what they want to happen, you'll ask them the third and final question:

QUESTION 3: "How can I help?"

____

[34] Michael Bungay Stanier, *The Coaching Habit,* 1st edition (Page Two, 2016).

This third question puts the postage stamp on your invitation to ownership. It's now in the mail, ready to be picked up.

Framing your response in terms of "How can I help?" tells them that they are in the driver's seat. You are just there to help. The decision, or solution, is theirs to make or find. Although you are willing to help in whatever way you can, this question communicates that you're not going to take over. You are asking them to give you directions that will help you assist them in solving *their* problem.

Do you see the magic in this way of framing things? By asking these three questions, you coach them to own both the problem and the solution, not you. This third and final question gives them the chance to take the lead in working out the answer.

Make these three questions a habitual part of how you lead, and you'll stop giving answers to every problem. As Michael Stanier jokingly says, you must learn to tame your "advice monster." A part of you loves to take ownership of problems yourself—that's how you got to be successful in the first place. But when you always take ownership instead of *leading for ownership*, you steal someone else's opportunity.

Instead, practice inviting others to ownership using the three questions. Let's quickly review:

QUESTION #1: "What's the real challenge for you here?" ("And what else?")

QUESTION #2: "What do you want (to happen)?"

QUESTION #3: "How can I help?"

Let me close with a word of caution: don't use invitations to ownership to push off significant problems or disengage when you're really needed. There is a big difference between coaching your people to take ownership using these three questions and simply saying, "Sorry, you need to take ownership of that problem yourself." The latter approach will only distance you from your teams, and it will probably make them feel frustrated. If a person is not already taking ownership of the problem, they need you, their leader, to help coach them along the path in a way that is truly supportive.

So quit your habit of providing all the answers and get in the habit of coaching your people to solve problems on their own, using these three questions. Look for an opportunity to practice this new habit today.

────────────────── **Take Action** ──────────────────

Stop Giving Answers

1. **Memorize the three questions:**
   - o "What's the real challenge for you here?" ("And what else?")
   - o "What do you want (to happen)?"
   - o "How can I help?"

2. **Create a visual reminder.** Write these questions on a sticky note and place it somewhere visible in your workspace.

3. **Practice self-awareness.** For the next week, each time a team member comes to you with a problem, pause before responding. Notice and try to curb your instinct to provide an immediate solution.

4. **Implement the three-question approach.** In your next three interactions when team members seek your help, use these questions instead of providing direct answers.

5. **Reflect and adjust.** At the end of each day, jot down how you used this approach and how your team members responded. Note any challenges you faced, especially in resisting the urge to give immediate answers.

6. **Share your experience**. In your next team meeting, explain this new approach. Encourage your team to provide feedback on how it's working for them.

12

The Best Way to Reinforce Ownership Is Through Recognition

*"People work for money but go the extra mile
for recognition, praise and rewards."*

- DALE CARNEGIE, author of *How to
Win Friends and Influence People*

The hallway buzzed with excitement as twenty senior leaders gathered for a high-stakes operations review. Danaher's divisional executive vice president was in town, and I was fortunate enough to be invited. When our GM presented our company's new product initiatives, he highlighted the 3D scanner project I had been working on tirelessly for months. He praised my dedication and ownership in bringing this innovative product to market. Heads turned, and I smiled sheepishly, but inside, I was beaming. That brief acknowledgment filled me with motivation and taught me the power of publicly recognizing people when they take ownership in their work.

This brings us to the fourth leadership practice related to the Invitation: recognize and celebrate people when they take ownership. By doing so, you actually extend another invitation for them to continue. When employees feel seen and appreciated, it inspires them to continue adopting proactive behaviors and mindsets. So, take the time to stop, observe, and express gratitude every time a person takes ownership of a problem. This sends a clear message that taking ownership is valued and celebrated.

This form of inviting others to ownership is especially powerful when you do it publicly. By recognizing someone in front of others, you not only reinforce this behavior in their own psyche, you send the message to everyone else in the room that the ownership mindset is welcome and rewarded.

However, while acknowledgment is a powerful tool, it has its pitfalls.

First, be intentional about spreading praise throughout your team. If only one or two people ever get recognized for how they take ownership, it can create a "teacher's pet" problem. Other people may begin to feel unnoticed or unrecognized, which can create divisions within your team. Repeated praise given to only a select few also can elicit the proverbial "hard eye roll" at the mere mention of taking ownership, and you may inadvertently create internal resistance to the idea.

A second pitfall to avoid is the temptation to acknowledge only the big ways that people take ownership. It's important to acknowledge even small and subtle ways that employees embody an ownership mindset. This communicates that even small acts of taking ownership are valued.

Leaders must recognize that not everyone's roles and responsibilities on a team are the same. The impact of proactive behavior is more obvious when someone has a significant role or a broad set of responsibilities. But by intentionally acknowledging the other, less noticeable ways that people take ownership, you reinforce your invitation to everyone, no matter the size of their position or scale of their responsibilities.

A constant challenge for all leaders is creating enough space to notice and recognize the positive things other people do, especially when you're feeling overwhelmed with your own duties and managing a large team. If you find yourself struggling to notice the visible ways people take ownership at work, don't worry. You can always just ask them. Then acknowledge their work and give them credit on the spot.

Another idea is to set aside time aside at the beginning or ending of meetings for the people on your teams to publicly recognize each other for the ways they've demonstrated ownership. This allows you to learn more about what goes on within your team, and it once again reinforces an ownership culture of OURS. The point is that recognizing and thanking your people for their efforts is essential if you want to continually invite them to take ownership in their work.

--- **Take Action** ---

Recognize Their Efforts

1. **Reflect on examples of ownership you've observed in your team**. Set a calendar reminder to do this for five minutes at the end of each day.

2. **Add a "Recognition Moment" to your team meetings**. Allocate five minutes at the start of your next regularly scheduled meeting for team members to recognize ownership behaviors.

3. **Balance your recognition**. Make a conscious effort to acknowledge both significant achievements and smaller, day-to-day acts of ownership across all team members.

4. **Implement immediate recognition**. When you observe an act of ownership, acknowledge it on the spot. Aim for at least one recognition every few days.

These practices will help you create a consistent habit of acknowledging ownership when you see it, thereby reinforcing its importance in your team's culture.

13

How to Clarify Responsibilities
for Maximum Ownership

"Accountability breeds response-ability."

- Stephen R. Covey, bestselling author of
The 7 Habits of Highly Effective People

At three o'clock on a Monday afternoon, I noticed our administrative assistant looked stressed out, so I stopped to ask if she was okay. She told me that she was struggling to pull the department's budget figures together before our four o'clock meeting. I was dumbfounded.

"Why are *you* pulling the budget numbers together?" I asked.

She responded, "Jim asked me to get them together before the meeting. I did it for last month's meeting, too."

"I didn't realize you were doing that now. Isn't that *his* job?"

"Well, it's mine now, I guess," she said, and shrugged.

On her face you could see more than a little frustration. This responsibility was definitely outside of her job description. Although her doing the task was a testament to her trustworthiness and competence, it was also a perfect example of how professional responsibilities can shift from one person to another without official acknowledgment or documentation. This can be a big problem if you're trying to create a culture of ownership.

Unless a person works within a very defined role at a large corporation, it's normal for job responsibilities to be in flux. People pick up new tasks and let go of old ones. This isn't a bad thing. Theoretically, if your employees grow and improve at their jobs, their responsibilities *should* shift. As people become more efficient and "able" within their current "response-abilities," they gain the capacity to take on new ones.

An ownership problem can occur, however, if people take on new responsibilities—or new "projects"—that are never formally assigned to them. Over time, an employee can accumulate a long list of tasks and projects that are now *implicitly* their responsibility but were never explicitly given to them.

When this happens, it creates two problems. First, there is a lack of formal recognition for work that is being done—and we all like to be recognized and rewarded for the work we do.[35] Your people are no exception. When they take on new job responsibilities, they want to be noticed and seen.

Second, whenever employees take on new responsibilities that are not formally assigned to them, they may be left wondering what level of involvement is expected. A default posture for someone in this position is to maintain the status quo—to do what has always been done. It is more difficult for someone to take ownership of tasks or projects that aren't officially under their purview because technically, in their own minds at least, the responsibility isn't something that belongs to them.[36] For better or for worse, it just fell into their laps. They may do it because you asked them to, but they likely won't see it as *theirs*, as something to own.

---

[35] Christiane Bradler et al., "Employee Recognition and Performance: A Field Experiment," *Management Science* 62, no. 11 (2016): 3085–99, https://doi.org/10.1287/mnsc.2015.2291.

[36] Elizabeth Wolfe Morrison, "Role Definitions and Organizational Citizenship Behavior: The Importance of the Employee's Perspective," *Academy of Management Journal* 37, no. 6 (1994): 1543–67.

That makes sense. When a task is not a part of what someone is "supposed" to do, it often feels like an extra burden, something to get off their plate as quickly as possible. It's unreasonable for you as a leader to expect that person to feel empowered to take initiative, make changes, or do things differently—unless you *invite them* to own the new task or project by formally and explicitly making it a part of their job description.

Now I can hear you asking, "Didn't you say one of the positive benefits of people taking ownership is the fact that they do things which lie beyond their formal job responsibilities?" The answer is, of course, "Yes."[37] But it is also true that it's much easier for someone to develop their sense of ownership within the boundaries of the specific responsibilities they have been formally given.

Factory workers do not take ownership of product sales or marketing strategy, nor are they expected to. Those activities are far outside of their defined roles. Instead, they own things on the production line, like safety, quality, or maintenance. It's much easier to own activities that are reasonably within one's place in an organization.

As a leader, you must get in the habit of recognizing when project roles or assignments change, and then ensure everyone on your team knows their responsibilities. Within those boundaries, you can effectively encourage and invite people to take ownership. Get in the habit of reviewing your team's *implicit* responsibilities and then converting those into *explicit* responsibilities, as defined in their job description.

This way, your team will feel empowered not only to take ownership of those tasks, but also to feel recognized for their work with the understanding that it is valued and important.

---

[37] Don VandeWalle, Linn Van Dyne, and Tatiana Kostova, "Psychological Ownership: An Empirical Examination of Its Consequences," *Group & Organization Management* 20, no. 2 (1995): 210–26.

Set aside some time this week to review your team members' written job descriptions and see where adjustments may need to be made. Next, initiate conversations to review these documents with each person to uncover where implicit responsibilities need to be made explicit.

Here's an added bonus: when you become mindful of your team's implicit tasks, it has the benefit of making your processes become more efficient. Often such tasks are either wasteful or can be eliminated entirely. Working to eliminate waste within each person's role is part of "job crafting," which is something we'll discuss in a later chapter.

—————————————— Take Action ——————————————

Make Job Responsibilities Explicit

1. **Schedule a job description review.** Set aside time this week to review the written job descriptions of all your direct reports.

2. **Create a discrepancy list.** For each team member, make a list of responsibilities they currently handle that aren't explicitly stated in their job description.

3. **Prepare for individual meetings.** Schedule one-on-one meetings with each team member to discuss their current responsibilities.

4. **Conduct role clarity conversations.** In these meetings:

   - Review their current job description and discuss any additional responsibilities they've taken on.
   - Ask if they do tasks that are not officially part of their role.
   - Agree on responsibilities that should be formally added or removed from their job description.

5. **Update job descriptions**. Based on these conversations, revise each team member's job description to accurately reflect their current responsibilities.

6. **Follow up**. Share the updated job descriptions with your team members and ask them to confirm that everything is accurate. Schedule a recurring task (perhaps every six months) to go through this process again.

By adopting this practice, you'll create clarity around your team members' roles and responsibilities, making it easier for them to take genuine ownership of their work and feel recognized for their contributions.

14

Why Collaborative Planning Boosts Collective Ownership

*"If you want to go fast, go alone. If you want to go far,
go together."*

- African Proverb

Have you ever noticed how difficult it can be to get yourself invested in someone else's agenda? Especially when you had no input? That was the position I found myself in as the incoming director of John Brown University's first year seminar program. This program was overseen by a committee of nine people, which included faculty and staff. About halfway into my first meeting, it became clear that there was a pre-set agenda that everyone expected me to implement. I didn't have any part in creating this agenda, and it was difficult to get invested in the work at first. Over time, I was eventually able to give my input to the committee and help shape our direction, but there was no invitation to do this at the start.

This is a common problem among leadership teams. Leaders involve a limited number of people when creating plans for their organizations and departments, despite what we've all heard about the importance of getting "buy-in." Most employees face a situation where they are given plans to execute that they had little to no part in creating.

To lead for ownership, you'll want to broaden the number of people you include in your planning processes. Doing so marks a significant "invitation" for others to take ownership in your department or company's goals and plans. It also helps foster a sense of collective ownership—that sense of OURS. Ideally, you create a recurring process for goal setting that involves as many team members as possible.

There is a common objection, however, to this ideal of collaborative planning. It goes something like this:

> "The more people you involve in a goal setting process, the longer and more complicated it becomes!"

There's some truth to that. Planning collaboratively requires an investment of judgment, creativity, and extra time. Adding more people to a goal setting or planning process can undoubtedly slow it down, but don't be limited by this thinking. Time is not your only valuable resource. You must also consider the quality of your plans and the ability for them to be speedily executed. When people buy into a plan that they've collectively created, it is more likely to be executed and to succeed. The downsides of a slower planning process are often offset by these upsides.

With that said, you can mitigate the slowdowns that can occur with collaborative planning in several ways.

The first countermeasure is simply to plan for it. Creating a culture of ownership among your teams and in your organization does require a time investment. This may mean you need to change your planning cycle, including your monthly, quarterly, or annual planning processes. But as mentioned, the result of having teams who can "own" your plans is worth the time trade off. Increased productivity, better execution, and faster speed to implementation outweigh spending a few extra hours or days each quarter to involve more people.

The second countermeasure is to work in smaller groups to narrow choices before involving others. For example, if you are considering five or more different strategic directions, narrow those down in a smaller group to two options before involving your wider team(s). Then get others involved in refining, shaping, and evaluating this narrowed set of possible goals and plans.

The key to this working, however, is that you must truly remain open to the options put forward from the group. If you or your leadership team have already made up your minds, people will sense it. Don't waste anyone's time with collaborative planning in that case, including your own. Ensure that your involvement of others in the planning process is authentic—otherwise, you will only damage trust and limit how much ownership they take on.

As long as you remain open and genuinely work toward a collaborative solution, you will not only get a better strategy, but you will also have far more people bought-in to the ultimate direction.

Finally, although major strategic goals are usually only set only once or twice per year, short- or medium-term goals can and should be regularly evaluated. Checking in monthly or quarterly on short-term goals can be a great way to give people ownership. You can ask them:

"Are we on the right course?"

"What's working, and what's not working?"

"What do we need to do differently next month to hit our goal?"

By asking these questions, you can let everyone in on some planning processes, even if your big strategic goals are non-negotiable. Involving your teams in these types of questions is a great place for them to provide input, and it makes everyone feel like they are being invited to take ownership in the company's success.

─────────── Take Action ───────────

Plan Collaboratively

1. **Audit your planning process**. List all your current planning activities (e.g., annual strategic planning, quarterly goal setting, monthly reviews). For each activity, write down who is currently involved. Identify at least two planning activities where you can include additional team members. Write down the names of team members you'll invite to these newly expanded planning sessions.

2. **Schedule your next collaborative planning session and prepare discussion questions**. Create a list of open-ended questions to guide the planning session, such as:

   - "What do you see as our biggest opportunities in the coming quarter?"
   - "What obstacles might prevent us from achieving our goals?"
   - "How can we improve our current processes to better meet our objectives?"

3. **Implement a feedback loop**. After the session, share the feedback and resulting plans with all participants and ask for their input on the collaborative process.

By taking action, you'll start to create a more inclusive planning process that invites ownership and buy-in from your team members.

FOUR KEYS TO OWNERSHIP

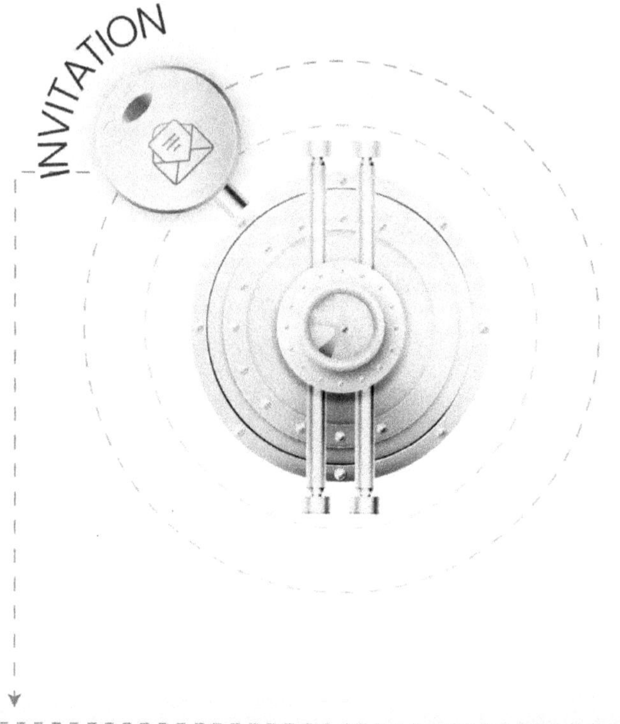

Key #1: Invitation

Actively encouraging employees to take ownership
of their work

Take Action

- Offer Ownership in 1-1s
- Stop Giving Answers
- Plan Collaboratively
- Acknowledge Their Efforts
- Make Job Responsibilities Explicit

Section Summary

Key #1: The Invitation

- Ownership is a socially constructed reality that requires explicit invitation. Regularly communicate your desire for employees to take ownership in their work, explaining what this looks like in their specific roles.

- Use one-on-one meetings to ignite ownership. Acknowledge progress, introduce the concept of ownership, invite collaboration, and commit to ongoing dialogue. This personal approach deepens the impact of your Invitation.

- When team members face challenges, resist the urge to provide immediate solutions. Instead, use the three targeted questions to coach them toward ownership, helping them develop problem-solving skills and autonomy.

- Acknowledge and celebrate instances of ownership, both big and small. Public recognition reinforces the value of ownership and encourages others to follow suit.

- Regularly review and update job descriptions to reflect evolving responsibilities. This practice ensures clarity and recognition, fostering a sense of ownership over both new and existing duties.

- Involve team members in planning processes to foster collective ownership. While this may require more time initially, it leads to better execution and increased buy-in from your team.

KEY #2
ACCEPTANCE

15

Key Concept: Seeing the Good Is Essential for Ownership

"Without a sense of purpose, no company, either public or private, can achieve its full potential."

- LARRY FINK, FOUNDER, CHAIRMAN
AND CEO OF BLACKROCK, Inc.

When the head of the world's largest asset management firm calls for a higher corporate purpose, people listen. That's what happened in 2018, when Larry Fink wrote an open letter to CEOs of public companies titled "A Sense of Purpose." With more than $6 trillion in assets under its management, Fink's company, BlackRock, wielded tremendous influence. So, when Fink urged corporate leaders to focus on purpose more than short-term financial gains, it struck a chord.

Although idealistic calls for companies to care about more than profits are nothing new, Fink's position at the apex of the financial world helped bring the message out of the periphery and into the mainstream.

As it turns out, purpose is a defining feature of a company's culture. A 2023 study on corporate culture conducted by Lighthouse Research & Development showed that the primary ways employees *experience* company culture are through its mission, purpose, and values. Runner-up categories included recognition, celebrations of work, and the company's approach to employee performance.[38]

These statistics are not surprising. The mission and purpose of a company are the ideals that define a company. They organize all the other activities into cohesive goals that are both good and worthwhile. Collectively, these ideals are of the utmost importance in determining whether and how people take ownership in their projects within your organization.

Why? Recall that taking ownership in any project means that a person has become personally invested in and "attached" to that project. Psychological ownership involves identifying with projects as MINE and OURS when people put their labor, creativity and effort into their work. People only form attachments to projects that they perceive as having good and noble purposes, and they remain detached from projects if they don't see them as worthwhile. This is a natural part of human psychology.[39] We only want to be attached to, and associated with, things that we see as good.

We've also said that attachment comes in degrees. We can be attached to some things more than others. In the case of work projects, a major driver determining the degree to which we become attached is just how *worthwhile* we perceive a project to be. We will not become attached to work projects to any degree unless we see them as having at least some intrinsic good. The more vividly this good is seen, the more invested in the project we

---

[38] Lighthouse Research and Advisory, "Performance, Engagement, and Culture Enablement Study," 2023.

[39] Psychologists have suggested that the pursuit of social worth is a basic human motivation, and philosophers from Aristotle to Hume have claimed this as well. See: Baumeister and Leary, "The Need to Belong"; Richard M. Ryan and Edward L. Deci, "Self-Determination Theory and the Facilitation of Intrinsic Motivation, Social Development, and Well-Being," *The American Psychologist* 55, no. 1 (2000): 68–78, https://doi.org/10.1037/0003-066X.55.1.68; David Hume, *A Treatise of Human Nature*, ed. David Norton and Mary Norton (Oxford: Oxford University Press, 2000); Aristotle, *Nicomachean Ethics*, ed. and trans. Roger Crisp (New York: Cambridge University Press, 2000).

can become. If we perceive projects as actually being bad for us or for others, or as unworthy of our time, then we won't become psychologically attached at all, even if we do show up every day for a paycheck.

> "To really 'own' a project, then, a person must "accept" the project as a part of oneself—as MINE and OURS."

To really "own" a project, then, a person must "accept" the project as a part of oneself—as MINE and OURS. People can do this by seeing a project's goodness. This principle lies behind all ownership and is the second Key to unlocking the ownership mindset.

One of your jobs as a leader, therefore, is to help employees see the goodness of their work. This can happen at two different levels. First, you can help them see the goodness of your organization as a whole. This means knowing and understanding the value your company brings to customers and to society.[40] This might include how your products or services improve people's lives, create delight, or make the world a better place. The goodness of your organization also includes internally focused evaluations—for example, that it takes care of its employees, pays fairly, behaves ethically, and does not discriminate.

Second, you can help employees see how their particular activities and projects connect to the organization's good. This means that each employee must understand how their specific job helps other people and projects within the company. Sometimes,

---

[40] The desire of employees to see the goodness of their work in societal or prosocial terms has been well documented. See, for example, Adam M. Grant, "Relational Job Design and the Motivation to Make a Prosocial Difference," *The Academy of Management Review* 32, no. 2 (2007): 393–417, https://doi.org/10.5465/AMR.2007.24351328; A. Colby, L. Sippola, and E. Phelps, "Social Responsibility and Paid Work in Contemporary American Life.," in *Caring and Doing for Others: Social Responsibility in the Domains of Family, Work, and Community*, ed. A. Rossi (Chicago: Chicago University Press, 2001), 349–99.

people understand the good their company does in the world, but they don't understand the value of their individual contribution.

To understand this better, I want to make a distinction between intrinsic and extrinsic "goods." In the business context, intrinsic goods are the positive benefits that customers experience *in virtue of your organization's products and services*. For example, if one is a home builder, the intrinsic value of homebuilding is that it provides warm and safe shelter and beautiful spaces for families to enjoy. That good is an inherent part of building a home and, by extension, of homebuilding organizations. These types of benefits provide "intrinsic" goods because they are part of the activities themselves, regardless of whether anyone earns a profit or not.

Extrinsic good, by contrast, is positive value that results from, or is a byproduct of, what an organization produces for the marketplace. This type of good includes making money, providing jobs for employees, or having a safe, friendly workplace environment. Calling this good "extrinsic" is not meant to diminish its value; it just means that it is not necessarily inherent in the actual products and the services that an organization provides to its customers.[41]

Earning money is an extrinsic good. It's also a great thing. Everyone in an organization should want to earn money, and lots of it—but money is always an extrinsic good, because it is something external to (or merely the result of) the good purposes of a project. If the reason people show up for work every day is *merely* for a paycheck, then by definition, they cannot be taking ownership in a project that is defined by your company's purpose

---

[41] Intrinsic and extrinsic goods therefore correspond to intrinsic and extrinsic motivation. Ryan and Deci, "Self-Determination Theory and the Facilitation of Intrinsic Motivation, Social Development, and Well-Being."

and mission. Instead, they are pursuing an individual project of making money for themselves and their families.

Working for compensation is not a bad thing, but because compensation alone does not draw us up into a *greater good*, it alone cannot be a long-lasting contributor to job satisfaction or retention. Research studies have shown this to be true, time and time again.[42] It's why many employees leave their jobs for the next highest-paying job. Money is only an extrinsic motivator. It doesn't keep people around. A raise will lift someone's morale for a time, but if that person is not invested in the internal aims and goals of your organization, they will remain personally detached and their motivation will eventually wane.[43]

For people to take ownership in the purposes of your organization—to become attached to and identify with those aims—they must see your company's purpose as good and worthwhile.

Your job as a leader is to regularly highlight and showcase the intrinsic goods of your company and the individual work of each employee. That's what unlocking the Key of Acceptance is all about: inspiring your employees to "accept" the purpose of your company as something they can care about, as something worth contributing to. They must then also see the connection between their daily work and the attainment of that good purpose.

---

[42] Tomas Chamorro-Premuzic, "Does Money Really Affect Motivation? A Review of the Research.," *Harvard Business Review* April 10 (2013); Anja H. Olafsen et al., "Show Them the Money? The Role of Pay, Managerial Need Support, and Justice in a Self-Determination Theory Model of Intrinsic Work Motivation," *Scandinavian Journal of Psychology* 56, no. 4 (2015): 447–57, https://doi.org/10.1111/sjop.12211.

[43] Money isn't the only possible extrinsic good of a project. As a former university professor, I met many faculty members who cited the time off and flexibility it afforded as their primary reason for staying in the job. Those external goods are why they stuck around, despite being personally detached.

Understanding the principle behind Key #2 is easy, but bringing it to life in your teams requires that you be intentional. The first step, of course, is to get clear, yourself, on what that good is. Only then can you communicate it to others.

———————————— For Further Reflection ————————————

1. Reflect on your organization's purpose. How clearly can you articulate the intrinsic goods your company provides to customers and society? How might you refine this articulation?

2. Consider your team members. To what extent do you think they understand and connect with the organization's purpose? How could you assess their current level of understanding?

3. Reflect on the distinction between intrinsic and extrinsic goods in your organization. How balanced is your current approach in emphasizing intrinsic goods versus extrinsic goods to your team? Are there opportunities to shift this balance?

16

How to Inspire Ownership Through Shared Purpose

"Great companies start because the founders want to change the world... not make a fast buck."

- Guy Kawasaki, author of *Think Remarkable*

Simon Sinek's bestselling book on leadership, *Start With Why*, stresses the importance of being able to articulate an organization's reason for existence—your WHY.[44] He makes a distinction between a company's WHAT, which include its products and services, and its WHY, which is the reason those products and services exist. He argues that most organizations know their WHAT, but that they struggle to find a clear WHY. In the context of talking about ownership, knowing both the WHAT and the WHY is critical if your employees are to see the goodness of your organization and understand why their projects are worthwhile.

According to Sinek, an organization's WHY is intangible. It is not identical to the value that you bring to your customers; rather, it answers the question of why you try to bring this value to them in the first place. The WHY elicits emotional reactions. The WHAT, by contrast, is tangible and does not elicit strong emotional

---

[44] Simon Sinek, *Start with WHY: How Great Leaders Inspire Everyone to Take Action* (New York: Portfolio, 2009).

connections. Sinek makes his point using the example of Apple Inc. About two decades ago, Apple's WHY was to "challenge the status quo and empower the individual." The company's WHAT included its lineup of computers, tablets, and iPods. Those devices brought great "value" to their customers. They were beautifully designed, powerful, and easy to use—and unlike Windows computers, they weren't plagued with viruses. But Apple didn't motivate their employees or acquire their customers by talking first about their WHAT (their products). They started with WHY.

Apple's "Think Different" marketing campaign illustrates how to lead first with WHY. Apple didn't showcase pictures of its devices. Instead, it showed the lives of iconoclasts—Pablo Picasso, Martha Graham, Jim Henson, Alfred Hitchcock, and more. This image-driven campaign made visible the invisible: it explained WHY Apple devices existed in the first place—to enhance creativity and originality, offering the opportunity for everyone to become a legend.

FINDING THE WHY OF YOUR PROJECT

So how does finding your WHY relate to seeing the "good" in your business project? There are two parts to understanding this. The first part explains how your products or services are good in and of themselves. This is their intrinsic value, or the WHAT. Your products might be well-constructed, enhance health, or make your customer's lives easier. Your services might entertain your customers or help them grow their businesses.

The other half of the story is WHY you produce your products or services in the first place. It's possible to make good products for bad or self-serving reasons, but an inspiring WHY is always for the good of others. It's about service and why you serve the people you

"If you're in leadership primarily for yourself, your employees will feel it."

do. Being in business merely to make money or build a personal empire is not a WHY that will inspire your people, even if your products do bring real good into the world.

It's important to recognize that a company can bring significant value to the marketplace, customers can love its products, and yet it can still fail to have a compelling WHY.

If lots of people buy your stuff, then you *are* delivering value. But why is your company in business in the first place? Do you know? Value can be delivered in neutral or egocentric ways, or in ways that serve others. If you're in leadership primarily for yourself, your employees will feel it. It will hinder them from fully seeing the positive potential of your company. If you or your leadership team implicitly broadcast the message that efforts to improve products and services are driven by money—whether that is to increase profit, get a bigger bonus, or to survive an economic downturn as an organization—then your WHY will fail to compel or inspire ownership.

This principle is true even if you appeal to an employee's self-interest when creating your WHY. "Everyone will get a bigger bonus this quarter if we do such and such" is ultimately a bad WHY.

Sales teams are often motivated by how much money they can make. Earning large bonuses or having huge upside commission potential are not bad things in themselves. But overemphasizing income can suggest to the employee that the "project" is a personal one aimed at earning money rather than a collective project designed to serve customers in the best way possible.

When an employee sees the WHY behind their projects as bettering the lives of customers or serving humanity, then even everyday tasks can "borrow" some of the good embedded in those greater ideals. People want to identify themselves with things that are greater than themselves. Having a WHY centered on others will inspire those you lead to take ownership in the work you do together.

A WORD OF CAUTION

We have been talking as if an organization's WHAT and WHY are totally distinct, but in reality, they are closely related. A good WHY must actually correspond to the outputs of your project—i.e., the products and services you produce. A good WHY cannot be so generic that no clear connection exists between it and the actual products and services your organization provides.

I once consulted for a printing company that was struggling to articulate its WHY. The struggle was partially because the company had so many WHATs. It produced everything from magazines and life-sized posters for professional sports teams to labels and packaging for baby formula. The company offered fulfillment, digital marketing, and a variety of other value-added services for its clients. The management team struggled to articulate the good of their company as a whole, mostly because they were trying to find a value proposition statement that included *all* of these products and services. They needed a WHY that would tie it all together and answer the question of why the business really existed. WHY did they make all these things in the first place?

The executive leadership team made an interesting move. In their struggle, they resorted to choosing a very generic WHY that did not connect to the intrinsic goods of WHAT they produced. They described their WHY in terms like, "Our business is about providing jobs," "We care for our people," "We provide opportunities for people to grow," "We are a friendly place to work," and, "We pay our people well." Their WHY was so generic that you could have applied it to almost *any* project or business.

Their proposed WHYs were, of course, all good things. And they did answer the WHY question, to an extent. But these types of generic statements were not connected to the printing tasks that people worked on day to day. That created a disconnect between actual work—operating printing presses, stuffing boxes full of pamphlets, loading boxes onto trucks—and the core WHY of the project. It was like asking an employee who was unloading a box of print supplies, "Are you unloading *this* box to provide jobs for people?"

If you make your WHY too generic, the innate human desire to do meaningful work will remain unfulfilled. Providing people jobs may be a part of the story of your business, but it's not *the* story. And therefore, it's not a good WHY.

VISION CASTING YOUR COMPANY'S GOODNESS

If your organization does not have a good WHY, you need to develop one. If you are a founder or CEO, you need to take this responsibility especially seriously. Even if you cannot determine a WHY that would satisfy everybody, you can still find a WHY that will inspire. Finding a WHY may take some time and feel tangential to daily business operations, but it is worth it.

On the other hand, if you are a team leader who hasn't heard a good WHY from your senior leadership, there's no reason why you can't create your own WHY and communicate it to your teams.

You must find your WHY. But you can't stop there.

Broadcast your WHY loudly and often. Many companies actually already have pretty good WHYs. Unfortunately, these live only on company websites or buried within mission statements. They are rarely communicated or reinforced. What most employees regularly hear about is the company's financial performance, so they start to associate financial performance with the WHY of the company. This has two consequences that will be detrimental to the culture of your organization.

First, unless your business has instituted a company-wide profit-sharing plan, most of the people in your organization do not have financial incentives directly tied to your company's performance. If you suggest making money is the WHY of your company, whether you intend to or not, this will disengage those employees. Since they cannot participate in a way that benefits them personally, why should they take ownership in a project that is now defined by making money? Why should they care? They don't, and they won't care about that kind of WHY.

For some organizations, "making money" is about survival. This is often true for companies in declining industries or markets, or those with very low margins. In such cases, leaders may attempt to motivate workers to work hard or innovate faster so that the organization won't go under—survival becomes its WHY, not goodness or serving others. Employees start to hear things like:

"If we don't increase profits this quarter, we may have to lay people off."

"If we lose any more customers, we may have to shut down."

Not only is this fear-based messaging a terrible way to motivate employees, but it also kills their sense of ownership unless they already have their own extremely compelling understanding of the organization's WHY.

Fearing for one's job security also has a secondary side effect: it weakens a person's intention to continue participating in your organization.[45] Without this intention, it's impossible for someone to take ownership in their projects (for more on this, see Key #4 on Intention). The natural inclination is to start making backup plans to find work elsewhere, and so begins their process of detachment.

---

[45] Cynthia Lee, Guo-Hua Huang, and Susan J. Ashford, "Job Insecurity and the Changing Workplace: Recent Developments and the Future Trends in Job Insecurity Research," *Annual Review of Organizational Psychology and Organizational Behavior* 5, no. 1 (2018): 335–59, https://doi.org/10.1146/annurev-orgpsych-032117-104651; Guo-hua Huang et al., "Deviance and Exit: The Organizational Costs of Job Insecurity and Moral Disengagement," *Journal of Applied Psychology* 102, no. 1 (2017): 26–42, https://doi.org/10.1037/apl0000158; Sang Hyun Lee and Dae Yong Jeong, "Job Insecurity and Turnover Intention: Organizational Commitment as Mediator," *Social Behavior and Personality* 45, no. 4 (2017): 529–36, https://doi.org/10.2224/sbp.5865.

A person cannot be fully invested in your company's projects and at the same time think that they will not be there in another month or year.

If your organization is fighting for survival, that's okay. But don't make the mistake of resorting to fear-based messaging or making survival your WHY. Instead, double down on messaging associated with your company's mission and purpose. Develop a clear and compelling WHY that brings to the forefront the desire to serve others. That, in itself, is a good reason to survive.

──────────────── **Take Action** ────────────────

Develop & Share Your Why

1. **Reflect on your organization's WHY.** Set aside 30 minutes to write down why your organization exists, other than making money. Consider how your products or services improve lives or solve problems for customers.

2. **Evaluate your current WHY communication.** Review your recent team communications. How often and effectively have you discussed your organization's purpose? Identify opportunities to incorporate your WHY into regular team interactions.

3. **Schedule a team WHY session.** Organize a meeting with your team to discuss and refine the WHY of your organization or department. Prepare questions to guide the discussion, such as, "How does our work make a positive difference?" and, "What would be lost if our organization didn't exist?"

4. **Create a WHY statement.** Based on your reflections and team input, draft a clear, concise WHY statement for your team or organization. Ensure it connects to your actual products or services and isn't too generic.

By taking these actions, you'll start to develop and consistently communicate a compelling WHY, helping your team members see the greater purpose in their work and fostering a sense of ownership.

17

The Best Way to Reframe Work

*"The first responsibility of a leader is to define reality
and the last is to say thank you."*

> - MAX DE PREE, author of *Leadership Is an Art*

It's difficult to take ownership in certain jobs, especially when you're doing mundane tasks like ordering supplies or filing paperwork. But William Pollard, the former CEO of ServiceMaster Inc., tells how this is possible. He recounts the experience of Shirley, a janitorial staff member in the company's hospital service division.

"Shirley sees her work as extending to the welfare of the patient and as an integral part of a team that helps sick people get well," Pollard said in an interview.

"As I talked with Shirley about her job, she said, 'If we don't clean with a quality effort, we can't keep the doctors and nurses in business. We can't serve the patients. This place would be closed if we didn't have housekeeping.' Shirley was confirming the reality of our mission."[46]

Although Shirley's activities were mostly everyday cleaning tasks, she transformed the meaning of those tasks by connecting

---

[46] As quoted in: Kenman L. Wong and Scott B. Rae, *Business for the Common Good: A Christian Vision for the Marketplace* (Downers Grove, Ill: IVP Academic, 2011).

them to a greater good. In doing so, she was also able to experience a strong sense of ownership in her work.

It's worth noting that Shirley saw her work as extending *beyond* even the mission of ServiceMaster itself. ServiceMaster is not a healthcare company, nor does it directly treat patients, but that didn't matter to Shirley. She was able to reframe her work as being a part of the hospital system and *its project and mission.* Shirley became personally invested in delivering excellent healthcare to patients. Thus, her "routine tasks" became "taking care of patients." The work itself did not change. The frame through which she saw her work did. Shirley was able to clearly see the value of her daily activities and take ownership of them.

Leading for ownership requires that you learn the art of reframing.[47] Although Shirley may have successfully reframed her work, it's unreasonable to expect that everyone can do this on their own. Leaders will often need to help people reframe their work so they can see its value and the contribution it makes to society or other people.[48]

Of course, Shirley had the benefit of working in a healthcare environment, and the good in healthcare is obvious. Depending on your field, you might have to use a little creativity to help your employees reframe their work in the context of a greater good. For example, a company that supplies component parts to airline manufacturers might help employees reframe their work as "helping the world travel safely," or "allowing families to experience the world's best destinations." There are a variety of

---

[47] Gail Theus Fairhurst, *The Art of Framing: Managing the Language of Leadership,* 1st ed., Jossey-Bass Business & Management Series (San Francisco: Jossey-Bass Publishers, 1996).

[48] The ability to reframe is also part of transformational leadership. Dean J. Cleavenger and Timothy P. Munyon, "It's How You Frame It: Transformational Leadership and the Meaning of Work," *Business Horizons* 56, no. 3 (2013): 351–60, https://doi.org/10.1016/j.bushor.2013.01.002.

ways to reframe the same work, depending on one's perspective and imagination.

Reframing becomes easier with experience, but there are a few places where your help might be needed. First, you may need to help people imagine the ultimate contribution that their work makes to humanity or society.[49] This is especially true if your company supplies goods or services to other businesses and the *ultimate* contribution or benefit of someone's work is further downstream in the supply chain. In such cases, you may want to help employees catch a vision for the positive impact of their work by pointing to products or services beyond those that your company makes.

Second, you may need to help people understand how activities and tasks are appreciated by others in your organization. Researchers refer to this as a task's perceived social worth.[50] When people see that their activities are appreciated by others, it helps them to see those activities as good in themselves.

If this sounds hard, don't worry. Reframing isn't something you have to do *for* your employees. It's something you can do *with* them—and it's a great topic of conversation for one-on-one meetings. When you have a reframing conversation, remember to be open and curious. One of your goals should be to learn about your employee's values so you can help them connect those values to their work. The point of a reframing conversation isn't for you

---

[49] This is sometimes referred to as "perceived social impact." Adam M. Grant, "The Significance of Task Significance: Job Performance Effects, Relational Mechanisms, and Boundary Conditions," *Journal of Applied Psychology* 93, no. 1 (2008): 108–24, https://doi.org/10.1037/0021-9010.93.1.108.

[50] Grant; Mark R. Leary and Roy F. Baumeister, "The Nature and Function of Self-Esteem: Sociometer Theory," in *Advances in Experimental Social Psychology*, vol. 32 (United States: Academic Press, 2000), 1–62, https://doi.org/10.1016/S0065-2601(00)80003-9; B. E. Ashforth and G. E. Kreiner, "'How Can You Do It?': Dirty Work and the Challenge of Constructing a Positive Identity," *The Academy of Management Review* 24, no. 3 (1999): 413–34, https://doi.org/10.5465/AMR.1999.2202129.

to give a prewritten script on how cleaning tasks keep hospitals open. It's to help people reach that conclusion on their own. The best way to do this is by asking open-ended questions about their work, the value they see in it, and the type of contribution they want to make to the world.

It will be helpful, of course, to have done this exercise yourself, first—but don't feel like you need to have all the answers. The mere act of having this type of conversation with employees can help them develop their own vision for the positive impact of their work, which will help them to accept it as their own.

Take Action

Reframe the Work

1. In your next one-on-one meeting, ask open-ended questions about how your employee sees value in their work.

2. Together identify one task they find mundane and brainstorm ways to reframe it in terms of its broader impact.

18

How to Connect Team Purpose to Organizational Goals

"Motivation comes from working on things we care about."
- Sheryl Sandberg, former COO of Facebook

Jackie is the new head of research and development at SolarTech Innovations, a company specializing in the development of renewable energy solutions. About a year after stepping into the role, she was confronted with a challenging situation: even though her team was composed of highly skilled professionals who were technically proficient and committed to their individual tasks, there was a noticeable lack of cohesion and enthusiasm within the group. The department's work was efficient, but it lacked a sense of shared purpose or collective ownership.

Jackie noticed a disconnect between the overarching mission of the company—to drive sustainable energy—and the day-to-day experiences of her team. They were aware of the company's strategic goals, yet struggled to perceive how their specific roles and projects contributed to the broader objectives. This disconnect resulted in a decline in team dynamics and a lack of personal investment in their work.

To address the issue, Jackie initiated a series of collaborative workshops. These were designed to involve every team member in discussing and defining the role of their department in relation to the company's mission. The goal was to develop a department-specific mission statement that resonated with the team's work and aligned with the larger corporate vision.

Through this process, a nuanced mission statement for the department was crafted. It articulated the critical role of the research and development team in achieving the company's sustainable energy objectives. This new mission statement emphasized the direct impact of their work on the company's goals and its global implications for society.

The process of creating this mission statement had a transformative effect on the department. Team members began to engage more proactively with their projects, demonstrating increased initiative and collaboration. They viewed their contributions not merely as individual tasks but as integral to a meaningful, shared endeavor. This shift led to enhanced productivity, increased innovation, and a revitalized team dynamic, illustrating how a well-defined, collaborative mission statement can help foster a sense of ownership.

As Jackie's example illustrates, many employees want their work to feel meaningful, but they don't readily see how the activities in their department connect to the company's mission or a greater good. As a leader, you can solve this problem and inspire employees to feel collective ownership by creating a group- or team-level mission statement. These statements help identify the purpose and significance of specific activities carried out by the people within your team or department. But before we get into the specifics of how to create one of these statements, there are three reasons why going through the process is worthwhile.

First, it's very common for employees to feel siloed within a department and isolated from the rest of the company. This can make it difficult to see how their department's work connects to the company's actual products or services, which in turn do good for humanity. For example, a mid-level accountant at a pharmaceutical company might struggle to personally connect with the company's mission to help people with diabetes. Even though he might know intellectually that his work contributes to this goal, it can seem far away and be hard to connect with emotionally. A group-level mission statement can feel more tangible and provide a bridge for employees to see their work as good.

The second reason to create a mission statement at the level of a department or division is to give people the opportunity to help craft the group's mission and purpose. The process itself helps them take ownership in the group. Typically, very few employees are involved in creating an organization's overall mission statement. It's usually determined by the founder, board of directors, or C-suite executives. However, you can involve entire teams in creating a mission statement at their level. This gives them a voice and makes it more likely that they will "accept" your invitations to ownership.

Finally, the collaborative process also fosters a sense of "we" among team members, which is vital for individuals to take ownership in projects as OURS instead of just MINE. By creating a shared mission statement, employees feel a sense of belonging and connection to their team and organization, which ultimately leads to greater engagement and collective ownership[51].

---

[51] Pierce, Kostova, and Dirks, "Toward a Theory of Psychological Ownership in Organizations"; Joshua Knapp, Brett Smith, and Therese Sprinkle, "Clarifying the Relational Ties of Organizational Belonging: Understanding the Roles of Perceived Insider Status, Psychological Ownership, and Organizational Identification.," *Journal of Leadership & Organizational Studies* 21, no. 3 (2014): 273–85.

HOW TO CREATE YOUR GROUP-LEVEL MISSION STATEMENT

To promote a culture of ownership within your team, a well-crafted group-level mission statement should achieve two critical objectives:

1. It should clearly express the *positive impact* the group has on the organization itself. This could be through its interactions with internal or external stakeholders.

2. It should articulate the *connection* between the group's outputs and how the organization serves its customers or society.

Unfortunately, many group-level mission statements fail to achieve one or both of these objectives. Below I provide some examples of second-level mission statements that do, however, meet both objectives. As you read them, pay close attention to how the group's positive impact to the organization is articulated *and* how it is then connected to the organization's overall good purpose. Underline where you notice this happening. Then, in the spaces that follow, consider ways that you might further develop these group-level mission statements if you were to make them your own.

(1) *Accounting Department at an Airline*: our mission is to provide accurate and reliable financial information that helps our organization make sound business decisions. We strive to ensure that financial reports are completed in a timely manner to ease the burden of decision making for our leaders, so that together we can help more customers get to their destinations.

What does this statement do well? Any areas for improvement?

(2) *Marketing Department at a Food Products Company*: our department creates meaningful connections to our company's customers through effective brand and product communication. Because we increase and deepen the relationships we have with our customers, we help more people lead healthy lives.

What does this statement do well? Any areas for improvement?

(3) *HR department at an AI Healthcare Company*: we support our employees' well-being and career development through training programs, benefits, wellness initiatives, and more. Especially with our large remote workforce, we strive to maintain meaningful and healthy connections between employees and an inclusive workplace where employees feel empowered for success. We know that a healthy workforce is key to delivering the next generation of AI technologies that will improve healthcare forever.

What does this statement do well? Any areas for improvement?

Which of the above mission statements do you think is best, and why? What are your critiques? It would be good to discuss these examples with your team before attempting to create your own. It is sure to prompt a productive discussion about what they would want out of their group-level mission statement.

If you decide to collectively create a group-level mission statement, make sure to periodically revisit it together. Get into the habit of referencing it when assigning projects and celebrating wins. If there is significant turnover within your group over a period of time, it may be good to go through the exercise again.

It's one thing to craft a mission statement. It's another to live it. Leaders must model behaviors that are reflective of the mission. Whenever the proclaimed purposes of a group are misaligned with actual priorities, ownership suffers. Although the process takes some effort, a well-crafted group-level mission statement can pay dividends with increased motivation and commitment. By clearly conveying both your group's impact and connection to the greater good, your mission statement can unlock the power of collective ownership.

Take Action

Go Two Levels Deep

1. **Schedule a team workshop** to develop a department-specific mission statement.

2. **Prepare discussion questions** that explore how your team's work contributes to the company's overall mission.

3. **Draft the mission statement collaboratively**, ensuring it addresses both the team's impact on the organization and its connection to serving customers or society.

4. **Plan regular reviews** of the mission statement in team meetings to keep it relevant and front-of-mind.

19

Why Success Stories Amplify Ownership

"Life's most persistent and urgent question is, 'What are you doing for others?'"

- Martin Luther King Jr., Baptist
minister and civil rights leader

A construction industry client blocked off half a workday for a longtime supervisor's retirement party. The celebration featured individuals from across the company, showcasing "before" and "after" photos of recently completed commercial construction projects, from high-rises and schools to massive apartment complexes. Children and teachers had schools. Families had housing. Businesses had new offices.

Until this point, people in one division had been largely unaware of the work occurring in other divisions, but now everyone in attendance was visibly moved by the images and the overall impact of their work. A growing sense of collective pride emerged as one person after another offered testimonials to honor a colleague who had contributed so much.

This event showcases the power of hearing, first-hand, how a business—as a sum of its parts—can change lives for the better.[52] Sharing testimonials from customers and internal clients is an incredibly powerful way to showcase the good your company does in the world.

But how do you collect these testimonials? It may seem intimidating, but it's important to recognize that if you deliver value to your customers, many people will be more than willing to talk about their positive experiences with you.

If you're in a direct-to-consumer business, your marketing department probably already collects (or has collected) testimonials for your website and promotional materials. Even if they don't, you can work with them to develop an ongoing process for collecting testimonials to regularly share with your organization and teams. Depending on your role, you may need to train other leaders to collect and share testimonials as well.

For companies that sell to other businesses, the best way to collect customer testimonials is by working with your sales teams. Partnering with them on this initiative not only gives them an important role in shaping your company's culture, but it's also a way of bringing departments together as a part of the shared mission. Just explain what it is you are doing and why, and then have them start to look for examples of recent "wins" that showcase how your products and services helped customers.

Many online services can help you capture data and collect feedback. Some newer tools make it easy to collect video testimonials, which are powerful ways to help people connect emotionally to the positive impact your business has on its customers. These video tools allow you to ask a customer, via a

---

[52] Nwamaka A. Anaza and Brian N. Rutherford, "Developing Our Understanding of Patronizing Frontline Employees," *Managing Service Quality* 22, no. 4 (2012): 340–58, https://doi.org/10.1108/09604521211253469.

video message, to share a short video post (from 30 seconds to one minute) about what your products or services mean to them. These can become great marketing assets as well as incredibly powerful culture-building tools.

INTERNAL CLIENTS

What if you lead a group or department that does not interface directly with customers, or you get resistance from your sales and marketing teams? Collecting video testimonials from "internal clients" can be a powerful way to go. For example, an accounting department manager can ask team members who work with financial reports to share testimonials about their positive impact on decision making. Internal client testimonials tangibly connect the work of your teams to other stakeholders in the organization.

Another strategy is the "get to know you" testimonial. Not every testimonial has to be a "thank you." For example, the leader of a maintenance division might ask people on the shop floor to describe their job. Sometimes, getting to know the daily work of your colleagues can be a powerful way to connect your team's work to a greater good.

MAKE IT A PRACTICE

Sharing testimonials must become a regular part of your leadership style for it to have impact. Develop a process for collecting and sharing testimonials and stick to it. Aim to share a new testimonial every month, if possible. Your people will love hearing about their positive impact. If you take the initiative to collect testimonials yourself, share them with your marketing department and you'll become their new favorite person.

To keep things fresh, mix up your forms of communication—email, video updates, and in-person sharing. Video updates can be shared via email by using services like Loom or mmhmm. The downside of digital communication, of course, is that people are less likely to talk about it together. Bringing your people together encourages discussion and builds a sense of community.

Here's one final trick, which I learned from a customer: invite people from other departments to share at your team meetings. This helps people feel connected to the larger organization and its purpose. Inviting a sales executive or marketing manager to speak for just three minutes at the start of a Monday meeting can be a great way to build community and cultivate a sense of OURS.

Sharing success stories and customer testimonials is a simple and yet powerful way to deepen connections within your organization and to reinforce a sense of ownership.

───────────────── Take Action ─────────────────

Share Testimonials

1. Reach out to one customer or internal client today to request a brief testimonial about how your team's work has positively impacted them. Then, share this at your next team meeting.

2. Schedule a monthly "testimonial share" and set the expectation that everyone comes to the meeting with something to share, either from a customer or internal client.

20

The Secret to Crafting a
Core Credo That Inspires

"If you can't write your message in a sentence, you can't say it in an hour."

- Dianna Booher, author of *Communicate Like a Leader*

My son Jack was diagnosed with plagiocephaly when he was about six months old. That's a fancy way of saying that he had a misshapen, flat head. Since I am bald myself, I worried that someday he might become bald, too, and I didn't want him to experience self-esteem issues in his twenties. My wife and I decided to use a custom baby helmet made by Hanger Clinic to re-shape his head.

In addition to these helmets, the company makes prosthetic limbs for people who lost their arms, feet, or legs. "Empowering Human Potential" is a tagline that appears everywhere in their clinic, along with photos of people who returned to sports and other activities after losing a limb.

The pictures are inspiring, but it was only after the third or fourth time visiting the clinic that I really understood *who* the photos and messaging on the clinic walls were for. They weren't there primarily for me, or even the other patients—they were displayed for the sake of the Hanger Clinic employees. Those posters create a workplace environment where people are continually reminded of the good work they do. This simple tagline, along with some compelling imagery, displays both the HOW and the WHY of Hanger Clinic and its service to the world.

This experience first taught me the power of crafting a "core credo." It's pretty common for a company's mission and purpose statement to be long and difficult to remember, and this is where having a core credo can help. It's a short phrase or sentence that succinctly captures the purpose or good a company delivers to its customers, society, and the marketplace. It serves as a focal point that reinforces why everyone shows up for work each day and captures the essence of a company's mission.

For example, one of our home builder clients came up with the phrase, "Building WOW Experiences" to capture the mission and vision of their products and services. This company's mission isn't just to build homes, or even quality homes—it's to provide astonishing (WOW) experiences that bring people joy.

If you want more examples, I've come up with some hypothetical one-liners that could apply to some well-known companies.[53]

Tesla: "Accelerating the move to sustainable energy."

Airbnb: "Belong anywhere."

Dropbox: "Simplify working together."

When developing a core credo, avoid placing the focus on your product or service. Hanger Clinic's one-liner was not "Helping people walk" or "Making limbs that feel natural." Instead, they made it aspirational. If your business sells to other businesses, you might want to have your core credo point to the final product(s) or service(s) in your value chain.

---

[53] These are examples only and have not been endorsed by the companies listed. I avoided using actual core credos to avoid trademark issues.

For instance, I know of a company that manufactures the small dial knobs (usually called "crowns") used in analog watches. That is literally their only product—these tiny little knobs. If they needed a core credo, they wouldn't want to say, "Building excellent watch crowns," or anything like that. Instead, a good core credo for this crown company would point downstream in the supply chain with a phrase like, "Helping the world keep time," or, "We keep time turning."

Does your company have a core credo? If not, creating one can be a great way to help your employees stay inspired and maintain a sense of ownership in their work. Just like the development of a group-level mission statement, you need to make the development of your company's core credo a collaborative process that includes many people. Then, use it and reinforce it often.

Take Action

Craft a Core Credo

1. If your company already has a core credo, write it down and reflect on its effectiveness. Use it in your next team communication. If your company does not have a core credo, think about who you would need to speak with, or get involved, in order to create one. Set a meeting with them for next week.

21

The Power of Visualizing
Your Mission

"Vision is the art of seeing what is invisible to others."
- JONATHAN SWIFT, author of *Gulliver's Travels*

Most everything we have discussed so far about the Key of Acceptance—mission statements, core credos, and testimonials—can be visually represented to employees. With the help of posters, signs, and other forms of internal and external communication, you can ensure that your employees are consistently reminded of your collective good mission and the value your company brings to society.

It can be challenging to capture the attention of your employees amid work demands and the daily deluge of information. Studies suggest that the average person sees between 4,000 and 10,000 advertisements per day, along with the constant stream of news, social media, and other distractions. This means that without an intentional internal communication strategy, your company's mission and values can easily get lost or forgotten in the noise. In fact, a recent management study showed significant gaps between what employees thought their company mission and values were and how they were actually defined by senior leadership.[54]

Consider promoting the mission and values of your organization everywhere people work, not just in the lobby. Display your aspirational imagery in hallways, conference rooms, and even the bathrooms. Remember, these visual signals are primarily for your employees, not your customers. If you develop a core credo, you can easily place that on business cards, email signatures, and posters. In short, don't be shy about promotion, because it helps to shape organizational culture. You have already put in the hard work of developing the assets. Now, make sure they are visible everywhere.

Many companies neglect their internal communications strategy or other culture-building initiatives because they don't see an immediate return on investment.[55] But culture is a key aspect of retention, and the ability for employees to perceive their work as good is crucial for establishing a sense of ownership. When employees feel connected to the mission and purpose of the company, they are more engaged, motivated, and invested in achieving its goals.

This wraps up the second Key to unlocking the ownership mindset: Acceptance.

---

[54] Irina Kopaneva and Patricia M. Sias, "Lost in Translation: Employee and Organizational Constructions of Mission and Vision," *Management Communication Quarterly* 29, no. 3 (August 1, 2015): 358–84, https://doi.org/10.1177/0893318915581648.

[55] Linjuan Rita Men, "Strategic Internal Communication: Transformational Leadership, Communication Channels, and Employee Satisfaction," *Management Communication Quarterly* 28, no. 2 (2014): 264–84, https://doi.org/10.1177/0893318914524536.

─────────────── Take Action ───────────────

Make It Visual

1. **Conduct a visual audit**. Walk through your workspace and note where you could add visual reminders of your company's mission, values, or core credo.

2. **Choose one visual element**. Select one item (e.g., your core credo, a customer testimonial, or a key value) to display visually in your workspace this week, and do so.

3. **Update your digital presence**. Add your company's mission statement or core credo to your email signature today.

4. **Plan a team discussion**. Schedule a brief meeting with your team to brainstorm creative ways to make your company's purpose more visually present in your work environment.

FOUR KEYS TO OWNERSHIP

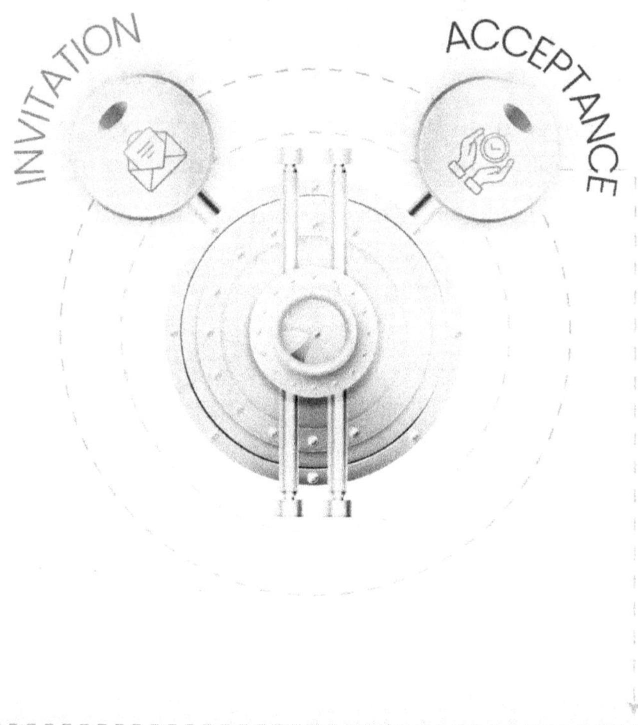

Key #2: Acceptance

Highlight the inherent value and purpose in each employee's work

Take Action

- Reframe the Work
- Share Testimonials
- Craft a Core Credo
- Go Two Levels Deep
- Develop & Share Your Why
- Make it Visual

Section Summary

Key #2: Gain Acceptance

- People only take ownership in projects they perceive as good and worthwhile. Help employees see the intrinsic good in their work to foster acceptance and ownership.

- Develop and regularly communicate your organization's WHY. A compelling WHY goes beyond making money and connects to your actual products or services.

- Create department-specific mission statements that link team activities to the broader company mission. Involve team members in this process to deepen their sense of purpose.

- Reframe mundane tasks by connecting them to their greater impact. Help employees see how their work contributes positively inside and outside of the organization.

- Regularly share customer and internal client success stories and testimonials to reinforce the positive impact of your team's work. Use various communication methods to keep this practice fresh and engaging.

- Develop a concise core credo capturing your company's purpose. Use it consistently in communications and visuals to keep your mission front of mind for all employees.

THE INTERLUDE: MASTERING THE ART OF OWNERSHIP

22

The Importance of
Shared Ownership

*"At some point, I crossed the line where it was no longer
about me. It's about us."*

- MICHAEL HYATT, former chairman and
CEO of Thomas Nelson Publishers

A marketing director at a financial services firm struggled to take ownership in a way that fully aligned with her company's mission and values. This person was excellent in so many ways and took complete ownership of her work, but her supervisor thought her sense of ownership had too much MINE and not enough OURS, which created stress in their working relationship. She resisted taking direction from him, especially when it came to using values-based messaging in their marketing campaigns. Ie eventually decided the company's messaging was beginning to drift, and he let her go.

Situations like these raise important questions for leaders trying to cultivate a shared sense of ownership in their organizations. Could he have coached her differently? Was he too controlling? Or was this just a case of "taking ownership" gone wrong? Often, in such cases, it's hard to tell.

The difficulties and tensions in forming a common sense of ownership are ones we all face, usually beginning early in childhood. At our house, for example, we keep a large set of Legos in a bin in the playroom for our kids to share, but my wife and I continually find ourselves having to explain to our children that the Legos are OURS—as in, they are owned *by the family*. They do not belong exclusively to any one person. Everyone can use them. Just because one of my sons builds a spaceship from the Legos doesn't mean that his brother or sister can't later use those same blocks.

Part of my duty as a parent is to help my children develop and cultivate a sense of shared ownership. In fact, learning to manage the emotions related to our ownership attachments is an important part of growing up and maturing as a human being. Aristotle famously said that man is a "social animal" by nature,[56] and learning to regulate our sense of ownership is a part of how we learn to function well in human society. It is possible to take ownership well, and to take it poorly. In other words, it's possible to be a good or a bad owner.[57]

In this section, we are going to switch gears a bit to dig deeply into that idea and provide a more nuanced view of the kind of "taking ownership" worth encouraging in the people we lead. We've discussed the ways that psychological ownership can go well and the benefits that it can bring, but I also want you to understand how shared ownership in projects can go poorly.

Part of getting ownership right is recognizing when we are in situations of common ownership. *Common ownership* is shared ownership (it's "OURS"), whereas *exclusive ownership* is not shared

---

[56] Aristotle, *Nicomachean Ethics*.
[57] Wilson, "The Virtue of Taking Ownership."

(it's "MINE," and mine alone).[58] Common owners must cooperate with each other and respect the wishes, needs, and desires of other people involved.

Sharing Legos illustrates many facets of psychological ownership, including the ways it can go wrong. Let's look at this psychology at play.

First, when I dump the Lego bin out onto the floor for my children, they find themselves with resources just sitting there, available for anyone to use. But as soon as one of them grabs a Lego piece and adds it to whatever they are building, it quickly becomes MINE in their thinking (psychological ownership). They feel this way because, as English philosopher John Locke describes, they have been "mixing their labor" into it.[59]

What is even more fascinating to watch is what happens when they actually do decide to build something together. They enter into what philosopher Robert Adams calls a "common project."[60] Common projects involve the cooperation or coordination of two or more people; basically, this is all organizations and businesses. To go well, a common project requires that people share a common sense of ownership, because it involves making something together. When my kids build a castle or a spaceship out of Legos together, it becomes a common project. It is then

> "When encouraging others to take ownership, we always want to do so in a way that emphasizes that sense of OURS."

---

58 For a discussion of over-possessive people who seek exclusive control in organizations, see J.M. Bartunek, "Rummaging Behind the Scenes of Organizational Change - and Finding Role Transitions, Illness, and Physical Space," in *Research in Organizational Change and Development*, ed. R.W. Woodman and W.A. Pasmore, vol. 7 (Greenwich, CT: JAI Press, 1993).

59 Locke, *Two Treatises of Government*.

60 Robert Adams, *A Theory of Virtue* (Oxford: Clarendon Press, 2006).

possible to observe them taking psychological ownership *in common* as they do this work together.

These simple observations about Legos can teach us important lessons about how we should lead for ownership. When encouraging others to take ownership, we always want to do so in a way that emphasizes that sense of OURS. We never build our teams, departments, or companies alone. Projects are always accomplished with other people, and they are always done in common.

This is important for leaders to remember as well. As leaders, it's common to feel overworked, underpaid, and underappreciated. To compensate for that, it can be easy to demand that other people respect *us* for the role that *we've* played in leading our teams or starting and building our companies. It's easy to lose sight of the contributions of others. There is a temptation to become psychologically attached to our projects as MINE instead of thinking of them as OURS. But seeing our work projects as common projects is part of what it means for us to be "good owners."

LEADING FOR "OURS"

What does one do when an employee seems to be overly possessive of their work projects, in the sense that they fail to appreciate it as OURS? One executive I interviewed told me about a product manager named Jill who was so invested in her upcoming product launch, she failed to recognize that it was just one project among the many competing priorities of the company. Others in leadership, and those on shared services teams, started to get frustrated with Jill as she pushed hard for her agenda. This executive had to have a gentle conversation that reminded her of the company's larger purpose, competing priorities, and the good work occurring in other departments. Without even knowing it, he was elevating Jill's conception of the "project" she was "owning" from a Level 3 to a Level 2 or 1. That is, he expanded her conception of what she took ownership in from being merely her product launch (Level 3) to the wider company's mission (Level 1). (For a refresher, see Chapter 6, "Owning Projects, Not Jobs).

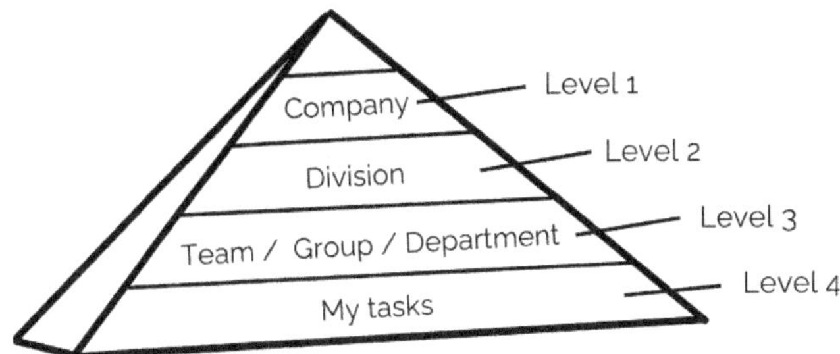

Sometimes, you need to have candid conversations reinforcing the collaborative nature of work. Remind employees that success stems from complementary skills and roles—it's not just about any one person's contributions. When having these conversations, however, make sure to affirm the sense of ownership that they do have and praise the positive ways it makes a difference on your team. In helping someone course-correct, you don't want to inadvertently kill their sense of ownership.

If someone wants to control all decisions or micromanages others in a way that stifles their autonomy, you may need to gently explain how these kinds of behaviors ultimately hurt the sense of ownership in others. If left untreated, the team will suffer. As much as possible, focus this type of person back to the team's mutual purpose and the company's mission. Encourage them to look for ways to empower others on the team and share credit. Although reasonable pride in one's work is natural and expected, repeatedly "hogging" responsibility or taking credit for everything is a sign that a shared sense of ownership is missing.

Finally, make sure to model inclusive language like "we" and "our" when discussing team projects. Publicly acknowledge every individual's vital role in achieving the broader mission. The goal is to cultivate a sense of ownership in common, where each person sees their work as part of an interdependent whole. Mature and healthy ownership sees beyond MINE to recognize what is OURS.

In the next chapter, I present a second way that ownership can go wrong. We'll discuss how someone's sense of ownership can be too strong, in terms of the degree of their attachment to work. Most businesspeople focus on how lacking a sense of ownership is a bad thing. But in addition to lacking a proper sense of OURS, a second way that taking ownership can go wrong is to take it to an extreme. We'll learn about that next.

—————————— For Further Reflection ——————————

1. Think about a recent project your team completed. How well did team members demonstrate a sense of shared ownership? Can you identify instances where individuals may have been overly possessive of their contributions?

2. Reflect on your own leadership style. How often do you use inclusive language like "we" and "our" when discussing team projects? Are there areas where you could improve in fostering a sense of common ownership?

3. Reflect on the balance between encouraging individual ownership and fostering a sense of shared ownership in your team. How might you adjust your approach to strike a good balance?

23

Why Extreme Ownership Can Backfire (And How to Avoid It)

"When a team takes ownership of its problems, the problem gets solved. It is true on the battlefield, it is true in business, and it is true in life."

- JOCKO WILLINK AND LEIF BABIN,
co-authors of *Extreme Ownership*

Mandy, a brand manager at a well-known consumer products manufacturer, leads a team that is developing a new household air freshener. Mandy wants to be a good leader, and she is committed to the project she's working on. She comes in early, works late, and does everything she can to keep the project moving.

Her teammates, however, describe her as too intense. She doesn't seem very open to other ideas, and she gets defensive when her own ideas are challenged. She often tries to take over tasks from others if she thinks they are moving too slowly instead of providing helpful coaching or other assistance.

Just last week, when her manufacturing colleague reported that the tooling they ordered would be delayed by six weeks, Mandy burst into rage, yelling at him right there in the middle of a meeting. When Mandy's boss found out about the "incident," he confronted her. Mandy left that meeting with her boss feeling utterly dejected. She was putting all her energy into this project, and now she feared (unnecessarily) that she might lose her job. Mandy's colleagues appreciate her efforts to a degree, but they also feel disconnected from her because she doesn't seem to recognize or appreciate other people's contributions.

Mandy suffers from over-identification with her work. Her unhealthy ownership attachment manifests in her behavior as well as her emotions. Outwardly, this negatively affects her ability to listen and take constructive feedback. Inwardly, her attachment leads to unjustified fears and an unhealthy conception of her own self-worth.

This isn't unique to Mandy. Research has shown that people can actually become ill or depressed—even suicidal—when they become overly attached to work and then are fired or let go, or when a work project fails.[61] As someone who wants to lead for ownership, it's important to remember that the goal of promoting a sense of ownership on your team isn't to overdrive performance at all costs. Rather, you want to create healthy, self-managing teams that actively take ownership of their work, while also maintaining a positive sense of personal identity.

TAKING OWNERSHIP AS A VIRTUE

Developing a mature and productive sense of ownership requires more than just having a personal attachment to our projects. To take ownership well, it must be done in a balanced way that considers a person's well-being and the team's long-term success. I call this the "virtue" of taking ownership.[62]

---

[61] Pierce, Kostova, and Dirks, "Toward a Theory of Psychological Ownership in Organizations"; Cram and Paton, "Personal Possessions and Self-Identity: The Experiences of Elderly Women in Three Residential Settings."

[62] Wilson, "The Virtue of Taking Ownership."

Virtue is a concept that comes from ancient Greek philosophy and the Greek word *arête*, meaning "excellence." Ancient Greek philosophers thought that virtues were excellent character traits, ones that make people "good" as human beings. We all know what virtues are, even if we haven't heard them by that name—courage, generosity, honesty, temperance, and more. These traits are considered virtues (unlike other personality traits, such as being shy) because they represent the *excellent* middle path between two extremes, and, lucky for us, they can be developed over time.

For example, courage is the middle path between cowardice and rashness. Generosity is the middle between being a miser and a spendthrift. Virtuous character traits cut a path between being excessive and deficient, and they embody a sort of right reason, or wisdom.

To take ownership well is to possess a certain kind of virtue, one that requires calibrating our investment in work appropriately. It means that we don't become detached and indifferent, but also that we don't become overly attached and manic about our projects. A healthy sense of ownership embodies the human longing to invest ourselves deeply into meaningful work, but balance is also needed to avoid the extremes that produce dysfunction.

> "To take ownership well is to possess a certain kind of virtue, one that requires calibrating our investment in work appropriately."

The following illustration shows how the virtue of taking ownership lies between being detached and disengaged in our work and being overly invested and excessively identifying with it. It is what Aristotle calls a "golden mean"—the appropriate middle between two extremes. As you may notice in the illustration, the detached mindset is shown as a larger area than over-investment. This is for two reasons. First, detachment and disengagement are more common and easier traps to fall into. When I train or run workshops with teams, I usually have leaders audit the people on their teams according to this diagram. Without exception, most team audits fall on the left-hand side of the scale.

Second, the "middle" way of a virtuous character trait is not like a mathematical mean. It is often skewed. For the virtue of ownership, having a healthy sense of ownership is closer to being over-invested in one's work than it is to being detached from it. This is similar to how courage is closer to being rash than it is to being a coward.

Figure 23.1: Healthy Ownership as a "Golden Mean"

Vice of Deficiency	Virtue	Vice of Excess
Detached Mindset	Healthy Ownership	Over-Investment

Strength of Attachment

None ⟵———————————————⟶

The extremes on each end of the diagram are the vices related to taking ownership. To understand what healthy ownership looks like, we have to know its extremes. Most of us are familiar with what it's like to work with those who are detached, and the negative side of that is fairly clear. The rest of this chapter, then, is about how to understand and deal with the other extreme: over-investment.

When people put too much of their sense of identity into a job or project, their self-worth can become dangerously tied to the project's outcomes. Constructive feedback can feel like a personal attack. Setbacks can result in outbursts of intense anger, or alternatively, induce an emotional sense of despair.[63] Such emotional volatility is personally harmful and creates tension with colleagues.

Being overly invested can also lead to possessiveness.[64] Those who insist on monopolizing key decisions often do so from an exaggerated sense of ownership. This can be the result of seeing a project as merely MINE and not OURS, but it also can be an outcome of over-investment.[65] A person's over-investment and over-identification with a project prevents them from recognizing and appreciating the contributions of others. It builds barriers rather than bonds.

Micromanaging, which we'll discuss in Chapter 25, is also a common result of over-investment. This is when leaders feel the need to maintain excessive control of a project. Too much command and control, however, destroys the sense of agency and ownership for others on the team.

Finally, no one can sustain the pace of overworking indefinitely. Burnout is the inevitable result. Not only can over-investment harm team dynamics, but it also takes a toll on an individual's mental health and personal life. For that reason, the ability to detach is critically important. Research shows that detaching from work after the workday has ended is important

---

[63] See Pierce, Kostova, and Dirks, "Toward a Theory of Psychological Ownership in Organizations"; Cram and Paton, "Personal Possessions and Self-Identity: The Experiences of Elderly Women in Three Residential Settings."

[64] Rochat, for example, identifies a range of "possession pathologies" related to having ownership which include "compulsive and obsessive behaviors like gambling, stealing, hoarding, excessive consumerism, and [excessive] debt accumulation." Rochat, *Origins of Possession: Owning and Sharing in Development*, 131. For a discussion of over-possessive people who seek exclusive control in organizations, see Bartunek, "Rummaging Behind the Scenes of Organizational Change - and Finding Role Transitions, Illness, and Physical Space."

[65] See Bartunek, "Rummaging Behind the Scenes of Organizational Change - and Finding Role Transitions, Illness, and Physical Space."

for mental health, well-being, and work engagement.[66] These same studies show that work programs aimed at improving the ability to mentally disconnect from work had positive impacts on stress, health, and performance.

Many people feel the impact of overwork. As someone who has erred on the side of over-investment, I have experienced many of these negative side effects myself.

EXTREME OWNERSHIP

The title of Jocko Willink and Lief Babin's bestselling book, *Extreme Ownership*[67], might suggest to some that taking ownership can never become excessive. However, an important difference exists between the "extreme ownership" advocated by Willink and Babin and the virtue of psychological ownership described here.

Willink and Babin's primary claim is that leaders should take complete responsibility for everything under their command—in their words, they should take "extreme" or ultimate ownership. There is no shirking of responsibility. No pointing of fingers. No one to blame but yourself.

Babin and Willink share many stories from their experiences as Navy SEALs that illustrate how a good leader takes responsibility in this way. Generally speaking, such responsibility is admirable. To take complete responsibility for your team and its outcomes is generally a good mindset to possess—it's certainly better than blame shifting and making excuses. But extreme psychological ownership, understood as an excessive attachment and personal

---

[66] Sonnentag and Schiffner, "Psychological Detachment from Work during Nonwork Time and Employee Well-Being"; Oakley and Cocking, "Professional Detachment in Healthcare and Legal Practice"; Sonnentag, Binnewies, and Mojza, "Staying Well and Engaged When Demands Are High."

[67] Jocko Willink and Leif Babin, *Extreme Ownership: How U.S. Navy SEALs Lead and Win* (New York: St. Martin's Press, 2015).

identification to one's work, can actually undermine a team's performance.

One must also be cautious about the idea of extreme responsibility. The desire to be responsible for every process can actually sabotage collective ownership in many contexts. Leaders who can't share credit can paralyze subordinates' sense of influence. On top of that, leaders who are overly attached to the current ways of doing things—because they feel extremely responsible for them—may resist necessary change and innovation. They may double down when pivoting is needed. This can cause blind spots and make one's strategy too rigid or stale.

Subtly seeking excessive responsibility and recognition can make the concept of being responsible more about personal identity than the shared goals of a common project. This isn't a criticism of Willink and Babin, but their leadership strategies can admittedly be easily misinterpreted or incorrectly applied to the workplace. In the context of the Navy SEALs, my understanding is that *the group* is of utmost importance and *always* takes priority over the individual. I only want to highlight the dangers of this type of "extreme ownership" in the civilian sphere. We must think carefully about what it means to take ownership well, and we must do so in nuanced ways.

CULTIVATING VIRTUOUS OWNERSHIP

If detachment and over-investment both prevent us from achieving excellence at work, how can leaders cultivate the golden mean of virtuous ownership? By far, the biggest problem for most leaders is how to get detached workers to start taking ownership. That is the focus of *Four Keys to Ownership* and this book. But let's also briefly address how you can support individuals like Mandy, who are over-invested in their work.

Work Detachment at Home

People who become over-invested at work may need help detaching from it afterhours. Research shows that a lack of psychological detachment during off-work hours is associated with emotional exhaustion, poor well-being, and reduced on-the-job performance.[68] On the other hand, practices aimed at improving one's ability to disconnect from work can have significant positive impact on well-being.[69]

Our family experienced this personally. After my wife became the medical director of the Siloam Springs Regional Hospital's emergency department in the winter of 2022, she soon found it difficult to leave her work "at work." She genuinely cared about her group of physicians and took ownership in the mission of serving patients. She also wanted to be responsive to issues as they came up, and she did her best to serve her team. But this also meant that work started to intrude significantly into her personal life and caused a lot of extra stress. After about 18 months, she began to feel burned out.

When a person successfully detaches from work in non-work hours, other important aspects of their life can play a more significant role in how they form their identity. In addition to our work contributions, people also commonly derive a sense of identity from family life, social interactions, friendships, and religious communities. Excessive work attachments can crowd out a person's ability to be present and fully engage in other meaningful parts of their lives.

---

[68] Laurens Bujold Steed et al., "Leaving Work at Work: A Meta-Analysis on Employee Recovery From Work," *Journal of Management* 47, no. 4 (2021): 867–97, https://doi.org/10.1177/0149206319864153.

[69] Tina Karabinski et al., "Interventions for Improving Psychological Detachment From Work: A Meta-Analysis," *Journal of Occupational Health Psychology* 26, no. 3 (2021): 224–42, https://doi.org/10.1037/ocp0000280.

As a leader, whenever you notice someone who seems over-invested at work, you can ask whether they are able to set-aside professional issues and stresses outside work. If a person doesn't do this well, you might consider an open conversation about boundary management and how you can support them. Many different strategies are worth considering, like setting rules around not checking emails after a certain time, leaving work devices like laptops at the office, or having rituals or activities that help transition people out of "work mode." The goal is to establish clearer boundaries and partitions between work and personal life.

Mindfulness and meditation programs can also help improve an employee's ability to be present and focused during off-work hours. With regular practice, people can learn to recognize when their mind wanders to work topics during personal time and build skills to redirect their attention in a non-judgmental way. This allows over-invested employees to detach and stop ruminating on work projects, so that they can be more present with family and friends. Your company doesn't need a formal wellness program to have this type of conversation. Many good mindfulness apps are available for free or a small fee.

Next let's talk about paid time off (PTO). Part of discouraging overwork means encouraging employees to actually rest and recover during vacation time. That means sending the message that, yes, it's okay for those emails to go unanswered. It's up to you, of course, to lead by example and foster a culture that does not reward overwork. If you are the one who constantly sends emails while on vacation or late at night, then you're sending a signal to your employees about what is expected and what will be rewarded in the long run. By discouraging after-hours overwork and normalizing taking "real" vacations, you can prevent burnout and give people opportunities to psychologically detach.

Finally, you may need to evaluate and adjust workloads. As a leader, part of the job is to assess whether employees have a reasonable amount of work that does not require constant overtime. Although some after-hours effort now and then is often a part of healthy ownership, it is usually not sustainable in the long run. If you see a consistent pattern of overwork for more than three months, you may need to reassess your employee's responsibilities, hire additional help, or redistribute workloads. When you lighten the cognitive load and time in the office, you free up mental resources for healthy after-work detachment.

Concluding Thoughts

Although it's more common for leaders to struggle with team members who lack a sense of ownership, it's important to be aware that people can also err in the opposite direction. Extreme ownership has its dangers, and to take ownership well requires that one find a middle path. At its best, virtuous ownership fuels creativity, initiative, and innovation. People stretch themselves to go above and beyond, but without the sort of over-identification that results in extreme emotional imbalances at work. We can care deeply while recognizing that who we are does not depend solely on work success. Then, when things do go well, it's easy to share credit with others for the team's success.

There's no doubt cultivating a culture of ownership will unlock your organization's potential, but for ownership to be sustainable and excellent, it must be understood as a virtue involving moderation. The goal of leading for ownership is never to get your people to invest themselves in work at all costs. Moderation will create an environment where everyone can do their best work and truly flourish.

For Further Reflection

1. Reflect on a time when you or a colleague exhibited signs of over-investment in a project. What were the consequences for the individual and the team?

2. Consider the concept of ownership as a virtue, with a balance between detachment and over-investment. Where do you typically fall on this spectrum, and how might this impact your leadership?

3. Think about your current team. Can you identify members who might be at risk of burnout due to over-investment? How might you approach helping them find a healthier balance?

4. Consider the difference between taking full responsibility (as advocated by Willink and Babin) and being overly invested psychologically. How might you apply this distinction in your leadership approach?

Section Summary

Mastering the Art of Ownership

- Ownership should be viewed as a virtue requiring balance, avoiding the extremes of detachment and over-investment.

- While detachment hurts performance and fulfillment, over-investment can lead to territorialism, micromanaging, and burnout.

- Cultivate shared ownership by emphasizing OURS over MINE in team projects and recognizing others' contributions.

- Help employees develop healthy work boundaries by encouraging detachment outside of work hours and recalibrating workloads when necessary.

- Foster a virtuous sense of ownership by connecting work to a greater purpose beyond personal gain.

- Leaders should model balanced ownership and help team members find their own equilibrium between personal investment and detachment.

KEY #3
INFLUENCE

24

Key Concept: Influence Is the Linchpin of Ownership

"It's feeling the sense of responsibility, the sense of ownership, to step in, to try to solve any problem."

- Laszlo Bock, former Google SVP of People
Operations and author of *Work Rules!*

Consider what you physically own: your car, your house, your laptop. Beyond the mere fact that you paid for them, what makes them "yours" rather than someone else's? The answer is simple: you fully control them. Within broad legal boundaries (for instance, stopping for red lights), you can use these items however you wish.

In the workplace and in relationships, however, influence—a more nuanced form of control that enables someone to have an impact—is central to ownership psychology.[70] Without influence, there is no ownership.

People must have real influence within their projects at work if you want them to take ownership. Your ability to help

---

[70] Jun Liu et al., "Psychological Ownership: How Having Control Matters," *Journal of Management Studies*, 49, no. 5 (2012): 869–95; Brown, Pierce, and Crossley, "Toward an Understanding of the Development of Ownership Feelings."

them achieve that *and* perceive it is the third Key to unlocking the ownership mindset.

There's an important relationship between psychological ownership and personal agency. In most cases, employees do not have legal ownership in the businesses where they work, so the kind of influence that supports an ownership mindset is not grounded in the *right* to control a project. It is instead based on a person's *perceived ability* to exercise influence over a project.

The exercise of one's agency must, of course, take into account that work projects are always accomplished with colleagues. Influence is always "mixed" with the agency of others, much as it is in the case of common ownership. No one has exclusive control over a project's outcome, not even the CEO.

> "Without influence, there is no ownership"

For this reason, "control" is not a good concept to use when we talk about taking ownership at work. The sense of "ownership" leaders want to cultivate in employees is shared ownership—projects that are always owned as OURS. It's similar to owning a vacation home with another person. Decisions regarding the home involve collaboration and can sometimes be complex. When someone starts to think of a particular project as exclusively MINE, trouble is brewing.

Another important point for leaders to understand is that turning the Key of Influence requires that you actually *want* your employees to have real influence over their projects. Many leaders don't. They want to keep control for themselves. But a genuine desire to give influence is necessary if you want to create a culture of ownership.

Likewise, many business processes are designed to provide a standardized way of doing things in lieu of personal agency. Processes are not a bad thing. But leaders must recognize that standardized processes effectively take away ownership. Unless one mitigates this effect by giving employees influence (and ownership) over the processes themselves, standardization can cause employees to detach both mentally and emotionally.

In the chapters that follow, I outline seven leadership habits or practices designed to help employees both experience *and perceive* that they have significant influence over their projects. The "and perceive" is important, because many employees *do* have significant influence over project outcomes, but they just don't recognize it.

The first three habits are soft skills that leaders at every level can work on. These habits strengthen employees' sense of ownership in their work by improving the quality of their working relationship with you. The remaining four leadership practices under this Key discuss ways to give people more influence by changing certain organizational practices—including, for example, the design of goals, budgets, and organizational structure.

Influence is by far the most important Key to unlocking ownership, and that means the top ownership killers involve undermining a person's sense of influence over their projects or organizations. Do you recognize any of the top five ownership killers on the next page?

TOP FIVE COMMON OWNERSHIP KILLERS

Influence is an ownership Key that most leaders can understand and appreciate. However, changing ingrained leadership styles is difficult. Below is a list of the top five mistakes, or "ownership killers," made by leaders and organizations.

1. **MICROMANAGING**. Micromanaging employees takes away their agency and problem-solving opportunities in projects, leaving them little influence over outcomes.

2. **TOP-DOWN DECISION MAKING**. Failing to include others in decision-making and goal-setting processes is a recipe for killing the sense that a project is OURS.

3. **FAILING TO LISTEN**. When leaders don't listen to ideas and input, they literally mute an employee's ability to have meaningful impact.

4. **NO FINANCIAL RESPONSIBILITY**. When financial responsibility is not given to those who should be in charge of budgetary lines, this weakens their ability and desire to take ownership.

5. **HOLDING ACCOUNTABLE THE POWERLESS**. When employees are held accountable for results that they are powerless to create, it creates bitterness and detachment.

BONUS: Soliciting feedback in meetings or employee surveys that no-one does anything about. This gives employees the impression that their voice doesn't matter.

What strikes you after reading this list? I think we all have experienced working in environments where these ownership killers were present. Take some time to reflect on your own experience and consider these mistakes, so you don't make them yourself.

———————————— For Further Reflection ————————————

1. Think about a time when you felt a strong sense of ownership over a project. How much influence did you have, and how did this impact your motivation and performance?

2. Reflect on your own leadership style. In what ways do you currently empower your team members to have real influence over their projects? Are there areas where you might be unintentionally limiting their agency?

3. Consider the "Top Five Ownership Killers." Which ones have you observed in your organization? How might you address them to foster a stronger sense of ownership among your team members?

4. The chapter emphasizes the importance of shared ownership (OURS vs MINE). How do you currently balance individual agency with collaborative decision making in your team? Are there ways you could improve this balance?

25

Why Micromanaging Kills Ownership (And How to Stop)

"Before you are a leader, success is all about growing yourself. When you become a leader, success is all about growing others."

- JACK WELCH, former chairman
and CEO of General Electric

Top MBA programs specializing in marketing teach students how to write creative briefs, which are detailed descriptions of the purpose and desired outputs of a creative project or marketing initiative. They define the brand's target audience, specify its tone or personality, and list any important elements for the marketing campaign, such as colors or logos. But the brief also leaves open space for a creative person to bring their specific ideas and talents to the project. The best marketers in the world know that excessive micromanagement of creative people quickly kills their output. It leads to uninspiring results and a frustrating collaboration. Good marketers understand that they need to rely on creative briefs when working with creative talent.

In my own time as a marketer, I learned firsthand the importance of giving creatives feedback without micromanaging them. The trick was to direct all my comments back to the brief without dictating specific design changes. If I ever found myself saying, "I want this element moved one inch to the left," or, "Please use this font instead of that one," it was a sure sign that I was about to kill the inspiration of my creative colleague. I was also killing whatever sense of ownership they might have had in the project. In my better moments I would give feedback like, "I don't think this element corresponds to the personality described in the brief. Please try again, paying particular attention to…"

Although micromanaging might get what I wanted in a more expedited fashion, it never produced the best results. The most effective way to give feedback was to explain why a design concept did not meet the brief objectives, and then *leave it to them* to find a better way to meet those objectives.

> "Micromanagement is one of the *worst* management styles if you want to increase job satisfaction and a sense of ownership on your teams."

The devil of micromanagement, of course, haunts more than just marketers. In one industry survey, IT professionals named micromanagement as the worst possible trait of a supervisor.[71] Micromanagement leads to low morale, high turnover, inefficiency, and team instability.[72] It is one of the *worst* management styles if you want to increase job satisfaction and a sense of ownership on your teams. Plus, being perceived as a micromanager can have serious adverse effects on your leadership progression.

Micromanagement is also a "sticky" behavior. A vicious cycle occurs when a manager who is already prone to micromanaging

---

[71] Zameena Mejia, "Tech Workers Say This Is the Worst Trait a Boss Can Have.," 2018, https://www.cnbc.com/2018/03/26/tech-workers-say-this-is-the-worst-trait-a-boss-can-have.html.

[72] Harry E. Chambers, *My Way or the Highway: The Micromanagement Survival Guide* (Berrett-Koehler Publishers, 2004); Namrata Mishra, M Rajkumar, and Rajiv Mishra, "Micromanagement: An Employers' Perspective," *International Journal of Scientific & Technology Research* 8, no. 10 (2019): 2949–52.

experiences poor performance from an employee. First, the manager begins to form negative beliefs about the employee's competency. Second, they lose trust in that employee. Third, the combination of number one and two make them feel the need to micromanage even more. Leaders who find themselves in this situation often feel that they *must* micromanage if they are going to get the results they need. And the cycle continues.

In theory, everyone knows that excessive micromanagement is bad—it stifles creativity, curtails initiative, and undermines trust between a boss and employee[73]. But so many of us still struggle to stop. For some people, it has become habitual, a part of their management style. Others micromanage only some employees and not others. Either way, the negative impact on teams is felt. In the context of our discussion, excessive micromanagement takes away a person's influence and, ultimately, their sense of ownership.

Micromanagers sometimes fail to consider that micromanagement is not just bad for employees, but also for them. Micromanagers spend more time at work stressed, frustrated, and feeling overwhelmed than those who lead for ownership. It is a common cause of burnout.

The solution, however, is not to suddenly take your hands off the wheel. Leadership expert Ken Blanchard rightly suggests that to lead well, one cannot take a one-size-fits-all approach to giving direction. How we direct others must be adapted to

---

73 Osmel Delgado, Elaine Mebel Strauss, and Melissa A. Ortega, "Micromanagement: When to Avoid It and How to Use It Effectively," *American Journal of Health-System Pharmacy* 72, no. 10 (2015): 772–76, https://doi.org/10.2146/ajhp140125; Feruzan Irani-Williams et al., "Just Let Me Do My Job: Exploring the Impact of Micromanagement on IT Professionals," *ACM SIGMIS Database: The DATABASE for Advances in Information Systems* 52, no. 3 (2021): 77–95, https://doi.org/10.1145/3481629.3481635.

specific situations—what he calls Situational Leadership.[74] He argues that in the realm of providing employees direction, leading effectively is task-specific and must be tailored to an individual's development level. This means that while micromanagement is generally detrimental, a more directive approach is necessary in some situations, which we'll discuss next.

Leading for ownership requires that you be willing to self-diagnose and adjust your management style based on both the situation and the individual. Re-establishing a sense of trust and adapting your leadership approach is critical if you want to give employees the real sense of influence they need to take ownership of their work. You can take four essential steps to accomplish this: (1) set clear expectations, (2) diagnose their development level, (3) adapt your leadership style, and (4) allow for growth and mistakes.

1. SET CLEAR EXPECTATIONS

We often feel the need to micromanage when we receive work from an employee that doesn't meet expectations. However, instead of looking inward at our own ability to set clear expectations, we tend to blame the employee for falling short. We see the employee's *lack of competency* as the root cause of the poor work, instead of our failure to provide them good guidance in the first place.

Whenever we do this, we mentally label the employee as being unable to produce results without significant outside help. The desire to micromanage seems justified, and thus, the vicious cycle begins.

When you fail to set clear expectations, your expectations are rarely going to be met. You then begin to assume that the only

---

[74] Kenneth H. Blanchard, Patricia Zigarmi, and Drea Zigarmi, *Leadership and the One Minute Manager: Increasing Effectiveness through Situational Leadership*, 1st ed. (New York: Morrow, 1985).

way to get the results you want is to meticulously "oversee" a person's work. This intense level of oversight causes frustration and detachment in the employee because they start to feel like they have less and less influence over their projects. It also leads to continued poor performance, as the employee becomes less motivated to bring creativity to their work. They know you're going to micromanage them anyway—and in doing so, you've killed the sense of ownership they might otherwise have taken. Down the spiral goes, until someone quits or is fired.

The first step to getting out of this cycle is to spend extra time defining clear expectations and instructions, setting deadlines, and selecting key performance indicators for every project you run.

In my experience, the failure to set clear expectations is often a result of not having spent sufficient time getting clarity on the desired goals and outcomes. Instead, we toss half-baked ideas to our teams and feel disappointed when someone returns with a work product that doesn't match our expectations. In my coaching practice, we use a specific tool called the Clarity Stack to help leaders clarify their ideas before presenting them to teams.

There are two critical parts to setting expectations. The first is outlining the deliverables; the second is setting firm yet realistic deadlines. It is common for leaders to delegate a task to someone on Monday, assuming it should take only a day or two to complete. They are extremely frustrated when Friday comes, and the work is still not done. The problem is that no deadline was set, so expectations were not clear.

There are two additional things to think about in how you set expectations. First, deliverables and deadlines should always be written down. That way you have a neutral document to point to at check-in meetings. Relying solely on memory is a recipe to build distrust when you and your employee remember things differently. Second, as you work to set better expectations for your team, make sure that they have adequate resources to meet the objectives you set. It's incredibly frustrating to be held accountable for something that's not in your power to produce.

2. DIAGNOSE THE DEVELOPMENT LEVEL

Once you've set clear expectations, the next step is to assess the development level of your employee for the specific task at hand. This is a crucial step that many managers overlook. According to Blanchard's Situational Leadership framework, an individual's development level is a combination of a person's competence (skills and knowledge) and commitment (confidence and motivation) for a particular task.[75] There are four development levels.

D1: (Low Competence, High Commitment): enthusiastic beginner

This person is generally lacking the specific skills required for the job at hand, but has the confidence and/or motivation to tackle it.

D2: (Some Competence, Low Commitment): disillusioned learner

This person may have some relevant skills, but won't be able to do the job without help. The task or situation may be new to them, or they may lack motivation.

D3: (Moderate to High Competence, Variable Commitment): capable but cautious performer

This person is experienced and capable, but may lack the confidence to go it alone or the motivation to do it well or quickly.

D4: (High Competence, High Commitment): self-reliant achiever

---

[75] Kenneth H. Blanchard, Susan Fowler, and Laurence Hawkins, *Self-Leadership and the One Minute Manager: Discover the Magic of No Excuses!: Increasing Effectiveness through Situational Self Leadership*, 1st ed. (New York: Morrow, 2005).

This person is experienced at the job and comfortable with their own ability to do it well. They may even be more skilled than the leader and can teach others.

It's important to note that an individual's development level can vary from task to task. Someone might be a D4 in one area of their job but a D1 in another. By accurately diagnosing the development level, you can tailor your leadership approach to best support your employee's growth and performance.

3. ADAPT YOUR LEADERSHIP STYLE

After gauging your employee's development level, you can adapt your leadership style accordingly. Blanchard's framework suggests four leadership styles that correspond to the four development levels.[76]

S1 - Directing: high directive, low supportive behavior

The leader provides specific instructions and closely supervises task accomplishment. They define the role and tasks and closely supervise the employee.

S2 - Coaching: high directive, high supportive behavior

The leader explains decisions and solicits suggestions from the employee while still providing guidance and direction. They offer encouragement and support to build the employee's confidence and motivation.

S3 - Supporting: low directive, high supportive behavior

---

[76] Kenneth H. Blanchard, *Leading at a Higher Level: Blanchard on Leadership and Creating High Performing Organizations*, 1st Edition (Upper Saddle River, N.J.: Prentice Hall, 2007).

The leader facilitates and supports the employee's efforts toward task accomplishment and shares responsibility for decision-making.

S4 - Delegating: low directive, low supportive behavior

The leader turns over responsibility for decision making and problem solving to the employee. The leader remains available for guidance but provides minimal active input, trusting the employee's ability to accomplish tasks independently.

The key, according to Blanchard, is to match your leadership style to the employee's development level for the specific task. For instance, a highly motivated new employee starting a complex project might need an S1 (Directing) style, with clear instructions and close supervision. As they gain competence, you might shift to an S3 (Supporting) style, still providing some direction but also offering support and encouragement. Your leadership approach can then grow with your employee.

This adaptive approach allows you to provide the right level of guidance without falling into the trap of micromanagement. It's a collaborative process—you work with your employee based on their skills and confidence in each type of work activity. You stop micromanaging, but in a nuanced way. Regular check-ins and progress reviews are still essential, but the nature of these interactions change based on the employee's development level and your corresponding leadership style.

4. ALLOW FOR GROWTH AND MISTAKES

A key component of encouraging ownership is allowing for growth, which often involves people making mistakes. Once you start empowering your people to make decisions and take risks within the scope of their responsibilities, they *are* going to make mistakes. Keep this in mind. Mistakes can be valuable learning opportunities, so resist the urge to intervene whenever you anticipate a problem.

For chronic micromanagers, this can be extremely challenging. When you see mistakes, your tendency is to start second guessing every decision someone makes.[77] Here's where you need to adopt a long-run view of your team and your organization. It's like good parenting. You can prevent your child from making mistakes and getting hurt by stepping in at every turn, but that's not going to help them become autonomous decision-makers as they grow up. Your teams are no different. Their long-term health may require living through some short-term mistakes, even if those mistakes cost something.

However, it's important to balance this allowance for mistakes with the understanding that each employee should be supported with appropriate direction based on their development level. For a D1 employee, you might need to provide more oversight to prevent unnecessarily costly mistakes, while gradually increasing autonomy as they progress to higher development levels.

When mistakes do occur, don't let your own sense of ownership drive you to fix everything. Instead, let your employees use their influence and agency to make things right. If you empower them *to fix the mistakes they create*, they end up experiencing a deeper sense of ownership in their work.

BREAKING FREE

Breaking free from micromanagement to create a culture of ownership requires deliberate effort, self-awareness, and a willingness to trust your team. By setting clear expectations,

---

77 Richard D. White, "The Micromanagement Disease: Symptoms, Diagnosis, and Cure," *Public Personnel Management* 39, no. 1 (2010): 71–76, https://doi. org/10.1177/009102601003900105.

diagnosing development levels, adapting your leadership style, allowing for growth and mistakes, and fostering self-leadership, you'll empower your team to take ownership of their work and create an environment where everyone can thrive.

Remember that leadership is not static. It's a dynamic process that requires continual adjustment based on the task and the individual. Effective leadership is about partnering for performance.[78] This collaborative approach to leadership can help you overcome stubborn micromanagement tendencies and foster a more proactive and capable team.

As you work on these steps, remember that leadership is a journey of growth and improvement. You're going to make mistakes. But with persistence and commitment, you can create a work environment that allows your employees to truly feel their sense of influence, while fostering both individual growth and organizational success. Embrace the challenge and watch as your team grows stronger, more capable, and more invested in their work.

---

[78] Kenneth H. Blanchard, Eunice Parisi-Carew, and Donald Carew, *The One Minute Manager Builds High Performing Teams: New and Revised Edition*, 1st ed. (New York, N.Y.: Morrow, 2009).

———————————— Take Action ————————————

Stop Micromanaging

1. **Self-assessment (Choose one):**

    (a) Keep a journal for the next 48 hours, documenting how you give feedback and intervene in your team's work.

    (b) Take our 10-question micromanagement quiz at ownershipunlocked.com/mmquiz.

2. **Seek feedback.** Ask a trusted team member for honest feedback on your leadership style, specifically regarding micromanagement tendencies.

3. **Situational leadership practice:**

    (a) Identify an upcoming task for a team member.

    (b) Assess their development level (D1-D4) for this specific task.

    (c) Determine the appropriate leadership style (S1-S4) based on their development level.

    (d) Write down how you'll apply this style to the task.

4. **Implement and reflect.** Over the next 48 hours, consciously apply your chosen leadership style to the identified task. At the end of this period, reflect on the experience. How did it feel different from your usual approach? How did the team member respond?

5. **Consider long-term support.** Based on this exercise and your self-assessment, decide if you need additional support to develop your leadership style, such as working with a professional coach or mentor.

26

The Surprising Power
of Active Listening

*"Most people do not listen with the intent to
understand; they listen with the intent to reply."*

- STEVEN COVEY, author of *The 7
Habits of Highly Effective People*

Several years ago, my wife and I worked with a marriage
therapist to help us communicate better and overcome places
in our marriage where we were feeling stuck.

During one session, my wife described some of the difficulties
in our marriage. The therapist turned to me and said, "Matt, now
I'd like you to turn toward your wife, look her in the eyes, and tell
her what you just heard."

"Uggggh." What *did* I just hear?

As it turned out, telling her what I had just heard her tell
me (the definition of active listening) was surprisingly difficult. I
was so involved in evaluating what she said that I wasn't actually
doing a great job of listening. In truth, I wasn't ever that great of a
listener, and it's something I'm still working on even today.

The importance of *listening* is often overlooked in business
training. The emphasis is often put on strategy, persuasive
speaking, how to make compelling presentations, or how to

negotiate effectively. But there is real power in listening—truly listening—to your team.

If team members feel their input is ignored or disregarded—i.e., they are not being listened to—they naturally disengage. That's because their sense of having any *influence* decreases, lessening their overall sense of ownership. The failure to listen is one of the top five ownership killers. It erodes the foundation of trust and collaboration on which effective teams are built.

The practice of active listening is an essential habit for leaders who want to lead for ownership. Let's first discuss active listening at an interpersonal level, and then I'll explain what it means to actively listen from the perspective of your organization.

REFLECTING BACK WHAT (YOU THINK) YOU HEARD

Many people first discover the practice of active listening in the context of personal relationships or therapy, as I did. But its application to business and leadership is enormous. As an active listener, you are not simply a passive recipient of information. Instead, you are fully engaged, carefully hearing and understanding what is being said. Then, you respond by paraphrasing back to the speaker what you have heard.

The act of restating or paraphrasing ensures that you clearly comprehend what was said. But even more important, it validates the speaker and confirms that their message was received and understood. It's akin to holding up a mirror to someone else's thoughts, allowing them to see their ideas acknowledged and considered. This validation shows that you care about what they are saying. Even if you don't get it quite right—as you often will not—active listening provides great opportunities for clarification and feedback, and this encourages open communication.

Let's take an example. Imagine that you are a marketing director, and one of your employees says to you, "I think we're missing opportunities by not being more aggressive with our online marketing strategies."

Now if you're like me, your initial reaction may be to *evaluate* that statement for its truthfulness, rather than first trying to fully understand it. You might think of a list of reasons why that statement is true or not. If you disagree, you may get defensive. You might counter with data that shows why additional investment into online marketing is not necessary.

But an active listener would respond differently, saying something like, "Okay, I'm hearing you. You think we could be more proactive in leveraging online marketing to capture additional opportunities. Is that correct?"

This paraphrasing assures the employee that you heard their idea, understood it, and are taking it into consideration. It also puts you, the listener, into a posture of curiosity, rather than judgment. By pausing and clarifying in this way, active listening allows space for additional clarification or elaboration.

Active listening seems simple, but it can have profound effects. Leaders who engage in active listening demonstrate to their teams that they genuinely value their ideas. It honors their input. This encourages team members to take greater ownership of their work because then they know that their ideas can affect the organization's decisions and direction. In other words, by active listening, you turn the Key of Influence.

But wait, there's more. Active listening also enhances your team's ability to problem-solve and innovate. By truly understanding the thoughts and ideas of your team, you inevitably make better decisions and incorporate more perspectives. This leads to better strategies and a more agile and responsive organization.

AN EXAMPLE OF ACTIVE LISTENING

Most of us who try to practice active listening don't get it right the first time. But the beauty of active listening is that when you don't hear something correctly, it's a perfectly acceptable result. The process of active listening itself brings further clarity to what has been said. Sometimes, it will elicit information that should have been communicated in the first place.

To see how this can occur, let's take a look at a project update meeting between Alex, a vice president of operations who oversees a large call center, and Taylor, a team leader responsible for upgrading the caller Voice over Internet Protocol (VoIP) system to incorporate new AI technologies.

> ALEX: Hi, Taylor. From your recent email, it seems like the team is finding it challenging to meet project deadlines due to unexpected technical difficulties. Can you elaborate on this?

> TAYLOR: Yes, that's correct. We are facing some technical issues. Our main problem is with the new software we're using. It's not as compatible with our system as we initially thought. It's causing delays because we're spending a lot of time troubleshooting.

> ALEX (first paraphrase attempt): So, if I understand correctly, your team is unable to meet the deadlines because you're spending too much time troubleshooting software issues. Is that right?

> TAYLOR: Well, not exactly. It's not just about the time spent troubleshooting *software*. Another big problem is that these software issues are causing unexpected setbacks in our workflow. We're having to redesign our processes and create workarounds because of the new software, which is causing delays.

ALEX (second paraphrase attempt): Ah, I see. So, the software compatibility issues are causing unexpected disruptions in your workflow, forcing your team to redesign processes, which in turn is causing delays. Is that a more accurate understanding?

TAYLOR: Yes, exactly. That's what we're dealing with.

As you can see, Taylor was not as clear as she could have been in describing the problem the first time. Alex first understood "troubleshooting" as concerning technical problems with the software, but he discovered through active listening that the software implementation created bigger-picture process problems. Alex now has a better handle on the problem and is in a better position to work with Taylor to find a solution and get things back on track. Taylor also feels like her concerns for the project have been heard, and likewise, she perceives that her voice has real impact on how the business moves forward.

INSTITUTIONAL ACTIVE LISTENING

The journey of active listening starts with practice. As you get better, you'll be able to inspire others to adopt the practice as well. But beyond your own listening skills, there is a crucial dimension of active listening that often gets overlooked—it's what I call "institutional active listening." The principle remains the same, but now we are talking about an entire organization (or a group or division) rather than an individual leader. In this case, the institution must echo back what has been communicated.

What does this mean in practice? Many organizations collect data through employee engagement surveys, climate surveys, and a variety of other channels. All too frequently this feedback is never adequately reflected back to the people who fill out the surveys. As a result, employees often feel as if their input falls on deaf ears. This sows further seeds of disengagement, as employees now feel that even their survey data doesn't influence the organization.

Institutional active listening, by contrast, involves two crucial steps. First, the organization must have a process to summarize feedback and reflect it back to employees. *This summary should include the full spectrum of the feedback received—both positive and negative, supportive and opposing.* This allows individuals to recognize that their input was heard, even if their opinions were in the minority, and fosters a sense of inclusivity, influence, and validation.

Second, leaders need to clearly explain how the feedback actually influences decision making, policy formulation, or any other outcomes. There's nothing more disheartening for employees than to be asked for feedback and then feel it is disregarded. Tragically, many leaders genuinely do value and integrate employee feedback into their decision-making processes, but they fail to communicate how employee surveys were used in that journey.

Institutional active listening, therefore, is more than just summarizing the findings of a survey. It's about demonstrating the impact of feedback on decisions. This is a vital step in reinforcing a sense of ownership among employees and creating an environment of trust and mutual respect.

PUTTING IT INTO PRACTICE

Active listening is a skill that you can turn into a habit. But like all good habits, it can be hijacked by emotions when we find ourselves in high-stakes or emotionally charged situations. It's much easier to actively listen in situations when the stakes are low and there is no real disagreement between the speaker and listener. Fortunately, there are a variety of ways to get better at active listening across the board. Here are just a few:

Self-Awareness Exercises. One of the first steps toward becoming an active listener is to understand your own listening habits. You can start by taking a self-assessment, asking for feedback from trusted colleagues, or reflecting on past conversations. Do you often find yourself planning your responses while someone else is still talking? Do you interrupt others? If you replied "yes" to one or both of these questions, you probably aren't an active listener. Being aware of your tendencies can help you identify areas for improvement.

Practice Paraphrasing. Paraphrasing is a key part of active listening. To practice, you can use everyday conversations or even content from books, podcasts, or videos. After hearing a statement or idea, try to rephrase it in your own words. This not only helps reinforce the skill, but it also can help you better retain information.

Role-Play Exercises. Role-playing can be an effective way to practice. You can do this with a colleague, a coach, or even in a group setting. One person plays the speaker and the other the listener. The listener practices active listening techniques, such as paraphrasing and asking open-ended questions that reflect an understanding of what has been said.

Mindfulness and Focus. Active listening requires focus and presence. Mindfulness exercises and other meditative practices can help train your brain to stay focused on the present moment, which is an essential skill for active listening. Mindfulness practices range from formal meditation and conscious breathing to simply paying attention to your surroundings. If you're new to mindfulness, resources such as the apps Calm, Headspace, and Breathe can help.

Active Listening Workshops. These in-person workshops and training programs are designed specifically to improve active listening skills. They typically offer a mix of theory, exercises, and feedback to help participants become better listeners.

Active listening, whether at the individual or institutional level, is a cornerstone when it comes to building a culture of ownership on your teams. As a leader, it's important to remember that active listening is more than just a management technique—it's a way of showing respect for the ideas and input of others. It promotes collaboration and cultivates trust. By being present, attentive, and responsive, you send a clear message to every person that their voice matters. This helps give them the sense of influence required to take ownership at work. Remember, a culture of ownership doesn't just happen—it must be cultivated and nurtured by leaders who listen, understand, and then act.

--------- Take Action ---------

Actively Listen

In your next conversation with a team member (within the next 24 hours, if possible):

1. **Practice active listening** by focusing entirely on what they're saying without planning your response.

2. **After they finish speaking,** repeat or paraphrase what you heard them say, starting with "So, if I understand correctly..."

3. **Ask them** if your understanding is accurate, and then invite them to clarify or expand, if needed.

4. **Reflect on how** this approach affected the conversation and your understanding of their perspective.

27

How to Make It Everyone's Problem

"When you're surrounded by people who share a passionate commitment around a common purpose, anything is possible."

\- Howard Schultz, former CEO of Starbucks

Have you ever heard someone say, "It's not my problem?" I think we all have. The *it's-not-my-problem* phenomenon happens frequently in organizations that lack a strong sense of ownership. It's most commonly seen when an issue surfaces in one part of the organization, and people in other parts of the organization don't care and don't want to deal with it. They may even say that out loud.

Having worked at universities for six years, I don't know of too many other places where this phenomenon is more prevalent. College departments tend to function quite independently from one another, and people often have very little view of the larger educational enterprise. This so-called "silo effect" within universities is a symptom of how people fail to conceive of their work projects as a part of the larger organizational purpose. If one college or department lacks enrollments, it's unusual for other departments to really care. Rarely do faculty take ownership in *the institution* as a whole.

To overcome this, leaders can use a method I call "connecting the dots." Remember that people take ownership in your organization at different "levels." The level in which they take ownership depends on how they visualize their "projects." Some people conceive of their projects narrowly, sometimes only within a department or a small team. Others see their work as essential to fulfilling an organization's very mission and purpose, and so they conceive of *their* project as identical to the entire organization. Remember, projects are just mental constructions, and people's perceptions can vary from person to person. (For a review, see Chapter 6).

As a leader, it's important to recognize that your employees often envision their work as contributing to a different "project" than the one you imagine yourself to be working on. Let's look at a few examples:

Example #1: An orthopedic practice

The physician-owners of a sports medicine practice imagine their collective "project" to be "helping people recover and get back to sports." The front-desk employees who answer the phones and schedule patient visits, however, don't see it this way. They conceive of *their* project as merely "I maintain the schedules for Drs. Brown and Smith." Nothing more. There is no greater good or end. They don't understand how their work influences patient care on a day-to-day basis.

Example #2: An electric car maker

The founder of an electric vehicle manufacturer goes to work every day thinking that her efforts are helping to "save the planet through sustainable electric transportation." A financial accountant at the company, however, conceives of *his* project as merely "producing monthly financial reports." In the accountant's mind, he doesn't understand how his work influences the production of electric cars. Maybe that's something the engineers do, but not him.

We should ask ourselves why the front-desk staff and the accountant view their work in such limited ways. What are the roadblocks preventing them from seeing their work as a part of a bigger (and more noble) project? The answer lies in two factors that shape how people conceive of their work. The first has to do with knowledge. The second has to do with *influence*.

The first way to enlarge an employee's vision for their work is to make sure they understand the organization's overall purpose. That means leaders must communicate that purpose consistently. Don't assume that people will just "get it" on their own. Without a shared vision, people usually default to a conception of work based on the outputs closest to them—e.g., producing the schedule, or creating the monthly financial reports.

The second way to expand a person's conception of their projects is to clearly show them the scope and nature of their *influence* on the organization. In the orthopedic practice example, when medical staff do not perceive how managing the schedule actually *influences* patient care, they struggle to conceive of *their* work as part of that project. That's true even if they understand clearly that the organization as a whole helps patients.

In the electric car example, the perception of influence also plays a critical role. If the company accountant does not understand how his reports are actually essential to making sound business decisions on the production line, he'll struggle to see his work as part of the project of making cars.

CONNECTING THE DOTS

To lead for ownership, you must connect the dots for your employees. If you want them to make *every* problem *their* problem, they must take ownership in a way that conceives their work as being part of the highest-level project in your organization. To accomplish this, they must clearly see how their work influences that project. It's your job to explain it to them.

In other words, what *is* the impact of scheduling on patient care? What *are* the ways that accurate financial reports are essential to achieving production goals? It may take some time to consider and find these connections. However, don't feel like you have to do this alone. You can do it right there together, with your employees.

To lead for ownership, make it a habit to remind people how their individual jobs influence the entire organization and its success. This can be done each time you praise an employee for work well done. It's a subtle shift, but a powerful one.

WHY TAKING OWNERSHIP AT THE ORGANIZATION LEVEL IS SO IMPORTANT

There's no moral wrong happening when employees take ownership in projects narrowly conceived, but it can cause problems.

First, it can make people territorial. If people don't see themselves as working on the same project as others—as defined by the organization's larger purpose or goal—then they will care about *their* "projects" more than they care about the success of "other people's projects" within the organization.

For example, if your marketing department launches a new product line, it requires coordination from other departments such as packaging, manufacturing, suppliers, and logistics. Now imagine that your packaging engineer sees *his* "project" only as "designing eco-friendly packaging for the company." If he takes ownership at that level, and nothing higher, then he won't care if problems or bottlenecks occur on the manufacturing or logistics side. This is the exact reason why so many people say, "It's not my problem." They're not taking ownership in the bigger project of the organization.

But suppose the opposite is true. Suppose the packaging engineer conceives of his work as part of the highest-level project or purpose of the organization. When problems arise within other teams, he will be invested in solving those problems, too. That's because he'll see himself as working on the *same* project and toward the same overall goal as other team members. When he's invested in the success of the whole, then he'll want to do whatever he can to help OUR project succeed.

WHAT TO DO: DRAW AN IMPACT MAP

One practical method to help employees connect the dots on how their work truly influences the larger organization is to create an impact map. An impact map is simply a diagram of causes and effects. It shows how an employee's routine tasks influence, positively or negatively (i.e., when done well or poorly), other people's work within the organization. Ultimately, you want the map to trace each employee's work all the way to the production of your company's products and services.

To make this activity collaborative and fun, don't do it in isolation; involve your employees in the process of creating this impact map. To save time, you can initiate the meeting with a partially completed map (or an outline) and then work together to fill in the remaining details. This interactive approach will provide an opportunity to discuss the influence of each participant's work. It allows people to vividly see for themselves how their contributions genuinely impact the organization as a whole.

Engaging employees in the process will have greater psychological power than simply showing them a completed map. Doing this exercise together fosters open communication, and it may give you a chance to learn more about issues faced by people in various roles. It also could be a natural complement to a job-crafting conversation, which we'll discuss next.

Take Action

Connect the Dots

Within the next 48 hours:

1. **Choose one team member** whose role might seem disconnected from the organization's larger purpose.

2. **Schedule a thirty-minute meeting** with this person.

3. **During the meeting**:
   - Start creating a simple impact map together.
   - Ask them to list their main tasks or responsibilities.
   - For each task, discuss how it influences other parts of the organization.
   - Together, try to trace at least one of their tasks all the way to its impact on the end customer or the organization's overall mission.

4. **After the meeting,** send a brief follow-up email summarizing the connections you both discovered.

28

The Best Way to Customize Roles for Maximum Ownership

"There are only two ways to influence human behavior: you can manipulate it or you can inspire it."

- SIMON SINEK, author of *Start with WHY*

Within six months of accepting my first job in marketing as a newly minted MBA, the economy cratered. It was 2008. My team shrunk from five people to just one—me. I was scared. I was also overwhelmed by my responsibilities. I spoke to my boss about the situation, and he asked me to catalog everything I was doing, including the things I *should* be doing that were not getting done. We scheduled a meeting later that week to review the list. I was a little nervous.

When we finally sat down together, his first question somewhat baffled me.

"What on this list can you stop doing today?" he asked.

I was confused. I assumed *all* the work on my list needed to get done. I had gone into the meeting assuming we would try to prioritize things, but to now think that I could just *stop* doing some of this work was a complete paradigm shift. Answering his question would require more time and thought.

Over the next few weeks, I identified parts of my job that I thought added the least amount of value. Working together, we eliminated those tasks and then prioritized the things that were of higher value. He also asked me to determine the best order and sequencing of tasks. Although we didn't know it at the time, what I had essentially done was a form of job crafting.

Job crafting—a term coined by organizational researchers Jane E. Dutton and Amy Wrzesniewski—describes a process where employees actively shape and redefine their job roles and responsibilities to make them more engaging and meaningful.[79] By giving them influence over the boundaries of their work, employees can align their jobs more closely with their personal values, strengths, and passions. The process has been shown to increase job satisfaction and contribute to improved engagement and employee well-being.[80] It also unlocks ownership.

> "Job crafting empowers employees to take greater ownership of their work because it gives them influence over their day-to-day activities."

Job crafting empowers employees to take greater ownership of their work because it gives them influence over their day-to-day activities. It allows people to exercise their agency and autonomy by giving them an opportunity to make meaningful adjustments

---

[79] Amy Wrzesniewski and Jane Dutton, "Crafting a Job: Revisioning Employees as Active Crafters of Their Work," *Academy of Management Review* 26 (2001): 179–201; Amy Wrzesniewski et al., "Job Crafting and Cultivating Positive Meaning and Identity in Work.," *Advances in Positive Organizational Psychology* 1 (2013): 281–302.

[80] Donald E. Frederick and Tyler J. VanderWeele, "Longitudinal Meta-Analysis of Job Crafting Shows Positive Association with Work Engagement," *Cogent Psychology* 7, no. 1 (2020), https://doi.org/10.1080/23311908.2020.1746733.

to their roles. The process is best understood by examining its three primary dimensions: task crafting, relational crafting, and cognitive crafting.[81]

TASK CRAFTING

Task crafting involves changing the nature, number, type, or sequencing of tasks that employees perform in their jobs. By identifying tasks that are aligned with their interests, skills, and values, employees can increase the senses of meaning and satisfaction they derive from work. Task crafting can involve adding new tasks, eliminating tasks, or reimagining existing tasks to better fit an employee's preferences. During the process of task crafting, employees analyze their current tasks and propose small changes they want to make to their roles.

RELATIONAL CRAFTING

Relational crafting focuses on the interpersonal aspects of a job, including the ways employees interact with their coworkers, supervisors, and customers. Employees can engage in relational crafting by building new relationships, modifying existing relationships, or adjusting the frequency and nature of interactions with others. This dimension of job crafting is particularly important for employees who thrive on social connection and derive meaning from relationships at work.

COGNITIVE CRAFTING

Cognitive crafting refers to the process of changing how employees perceive the tasks and relationships within their job. Employees

---

[81] Evangelina Demerouti, "Design Your Own Job Through Job Crafting," *European Psychologist* 19 (2014): 237–47.

can engage in cognitive crafting by reframing their understanding of their job's purpose, significance, or impact. This dimension of job crafting can be particularly powerful, as it allows employees to find meaning in their work without necessarily changing the tasks or relationships themselves. Cognitive crafting is actually what we are doing when we reframe an employee's work (see Chapter 17) or help them to connect the dots (see Chapter 27), as we discussed in previous chapters.

JOB CRAFTING FOR A SENSE OF OWNERSHIP

Job crafting can dramatically improve an employee's sense of ownership because it allows them to influence their work by putting their fingerprint on it. The process creates a greater sense of connection and attachment to the projects they work on. The job-crafting process increases one's agency by allowing a person to see themselves as the architects of their work environment, rather than merely as passive recipients of predefined job roles.

Let's look at a case study that shows how the principles of job crafting can be put into practice.

Case Study: Job Crafting for a Marketing Specialist

John is a marketing specialist at a mid-sized manufacturing firm. He has been working at his company for three years now, and he has shown great potential in his role. However, he recently expressed feelings of dissatisfaction with his job. His manager, Sarah, decided to explore job crafting as a way to rekindle John's passion for his work and to help him take greater ownership of his role.

Step 1: Identifying Opportunities for Crafting. To begin the job crafting process, Sarah scheduled a meeting with John to discuss his interests, strengths, and areas where he would like to grow.

John said he had a strong interest in graphic design, and he would love to be more involved in the creative aspects of marketing. He also mentioned that he enjoyed mentoring and working with junior team members. Based on this feedback, Sarah and John explored the three dimensions of job crafting, one at a time.

Here were the results:

(i)   *Task Crafting*

Sarah and John discussed ways to modify John's job responsibilities to better align with his interests. They decided that John would take on additional responsibilities in graphic design, such as creating visual content for social media campaigns and designing marketing materials. They also agreed that John would play a more active role in training and mentoring new hires in their department.

(ii)   *Relational Crafting*

To address John's interest in building stronger relationships within the team, Sarah and John explored opportunities for him to collaborate more closely with colleagues. They decided John could attend weekly brainstorming sessions with the creative team and partner with a junior marketing specialist on a project-by-project basis to provide guidance and support, as needed.

(iii) *Cognitive Crafting*

In addition to adjusting his tasks and relationships, Sarah and John discussed ways to reframe his understanding of his role and its impact on the company. Sarah emphasized the importance of John's role in shaping the company's brand identity and the value of his mentorship in nurturing the next generation of marketing talent.

Step 2: Implementation. With the job-crafting plan in place, Sarah and John worked together to implement these changes to his role. They communicated the adjustments to the relevant stakeholders, including John's teammates, and ensured that John had the necessary resources and support to succeed in his new responsibilities.

Step 3: Evaluation and Adaptation. After several months, Sarah scheduled a one-on-one conversation with John to evaluate how the changes were going. They discussed John's experience with the job-crafting process and whether the changes allowed him to take more ownership of his role. They also explored any additional tweaks that might be needed.

During this follow-up conversation, John suggested that he would like to take on more responsibility in developing the overall marketing strategy for the company, saying he felt that his creative expertise could bring a fresh perspective to the strategic planning process. Sarah agreed to explore this possibility and work with John on identifying opportunities for him to contribute to the marketing strategy going forward.

John's example illustrates how job crafting can be a highly effective method for managers to help employees take ownership of their work and find greater meaning and satisfaction in their roles. By understanding and addressing the unique strengths, interests, and goals of each employee through this structured, three-step process, leaders can create a more engaged and passionate workforce that is better equipped to take ownership and drive success.

──────────────── Take Action ────────────────

Job Crafting

While comprehensive job crafting can be an extensive process and is often best facilitated by an outside consultant, you can still initiate meaningful change through a simplified job-crafting session. Here's how to get started:

1. **Within the next week**, choose one team member for a job-crafting conversation.

2. **Schedule a 45- to 60-minute meeting** with this person.

3. **Before the meeting**, ask them to reflect on:
    o Tasks they enjoy most and least in their current role.
    o Skills they'd like to develop or use more.
    o Relationships they'd like to build or strengthen at work.

4. **During the meeting**:
    o Discuss their reflections.
    o Explore at least one change in each area of job crafting together:
        1. Task crafting. Identify one task to add, modify, or remove.
        2. Relational crafting. Find one way to adjust their work relationships.
        3. Cognitive crafting. Discuss how to reframe one aspect of their role.

5. **Agree on a small, immediate change** to implement within the next two weeks.

6. **Schedule a follow-up meeting** to review the impact of these changes.

29

Why Flattening Hierarchy
Boosts Ownership

*"Leadership is about solving problems and changing
the order of things for the better."*

- CARLY FIORINA, former CEO of Hewlett-Packard

I once joined an organization that, on the surface, seemed relatively flat in terms of its hierarchy; only two levels separated the company president from most of the employees. But after about nine months of working there, it became clear that things were extremely hierarchical when it came to decision making. The president held the reins and left little room for others to exercise their judgment.

The impact was palpable: innovation, morale, and engagement all suffered. I noticed this particularly among people who had been there for at least three years. They had learned from experience that their input was rarely taken seriously, and the decisions they made would likely be overridden with new initiatives, which were always tightly controlled. They felt they had little real power or influence.

This not only eroded their sense of ownership, but it also created a general apathy, and in some cases, resentment. I noticed that whenever the president threw out a question at one of his monthly large-group meetings, it was almost always met with crickets. Everyone's sense of agency had been undermined by a centralized decision-making structure.

Organizational hierarchy can take several forms, and it's important that we distinguish them. First, we are all familiar with what one might call "structural hierarchy;" that is the multi-tiered organizational chart that reaches from the CEO all the way down to entry-level employees. Structural hierarchy is symbolized by the chart of responsibilities in an organization. It's how we typically think of business hierarchies.

Evaluating structural hierarchies within an organization is crucial. But even more important to understand is an organization's decision-making hierarchy, especially when we're thinking about ownership. The decision-making hierarchy is often informal and doesn't play by the rules as documented in the official org chart. It's about who really gets to make meaningful decisions.

Resisting both types of hierarchy within your organization is essential if you are going to foster a sense of ownership among employees. By involving employees in decision-making processes, you give them a real way to influence their projects. This not only encourages innovation[82] and creativity, but it also enhances commitment.[83]

If your organization has many levels, developing a collective sense of ownership is going to take more than just increasing the number of people involved in decision-making processes. Other changes will likely be required to effectively support decision making at lower levels in the organization.

---

[82] R.M. Kanter, "The Middle Manager as Innovator," *Harvard Business Review* July-August (2004): 150–60.

[83] Xu Huang et al., "Does Participative Leadership Enhance Work Performance by Inducing Empowerment or Trust? The Differential Effects on Managerial and Non-Managerial Subordinates," *Journal of Organizational Behavior* 31, no. 1 (2010): 122–43, https://doi.org/10.1002/job.636.

Consider the structural and psychological aspects of your organization—you may need to reevaluate them as you look to resist hierarchy and give influence and ownership to your teams. These aspects include:

Transparency. If your organization is hierarchical, it's likely that valuable information is held by only top management or certain departments. This siloed approach will hinder informed decision making. You'll want to consider increasing transparency—making information readily available to all members of your organization—as you empower your teams to make decisions.[84] If you want people to think and act like owners, you need to give them the kind of information that owners get. This might involve sharing financial reports, company metrics, and being more open about the company's challenges and successes.

Psychological Safety. Psychological safety is a term coined by Harvard University's Amy Edmondson. Edmonson, a professor of leadership and management who studies teaming and organizational learning, defines psychological safety as a shared belief that a team or organization is a safe place for interpersonal risk taking.[85] In a psychologically safe team, members feel accepted despite their imperfections, and they know ideas will be respected even when they differ. When people feel psychologically safe, they are more comfortable taking risks and making mistakes, knowing that they will not be punished or humiliated. This type of environment is crucial if you want employees to take responsibility for decision making, especially when it's new to

---

[84] Andrew K. Schnackenberg and Edward C. Tomlinson, "Organizational Transparency: A New Perspective on Managing Trust in Organization-Stakeholder Relationships," *Journal of Management* 42, no. 7 (2016): 1784–1810, https://doi.org/10.1177/0149206314525202.

[85] Amy C. Edmondson, *The Fearless Organization: Creating Psychological Safety in the Workplace for Learning, Innovation, and Growth* (Hoboken, N.J.: Wiley, 2019).

them. To foster psychological safety, it's important to encourage open communication, allow for mistakes, and promote a no-blame culture. (Check out Dr. Edmondson's book, *The Fearless Organization*, as a great place to start.)

Training and Development. Training and development are key to equipping teams with the necessary skills and knowledge to make informed decisions and take on new responsibilities. This includes both technical skills related to their specific roles and soft skills like communication, leadership, and problem-solving.

Often leadership training is neglected when people are promoted from individual contributor to management roles. It's also commonly overlooked when promoting a manager to become a leader of other managers.[86] This results in bad leadership, which ultimately leads to a lack of trust among senior leaders and a resistance to empowering others with decision-making authority. The problem is not the people, however—it's the lack of training by the organization. By offering training opportunities and leadership development, you can enhance employees' confidence in their abilities and increase their willingness to make decisions and take ownership of their work.

DECENTRALIZATION REQUIRES TRUST AND DECISION-MAKING POWER

Resisting hierarchy and decentralizing organizational decision-making is a powerful way to foster ownership among teams. By recognizing and addressing how decisions are made within your organization, you can release control where appropriate and

---

[86] Ram Charan, *The Leadership Pipeline: How to Build the Leadership Powered Company*, 2nd ed., J-B US Non-Franchise Leadership (San Francisco, California: Jossey-Bass, 2011).

pave the way for greater engagement, innovation, and improved morale.

At its heart, resisting hierarchy is about trust. It's about trusting your team with information, trusting them to make and learn from mistakes, and trusting them to take on new responsibilities. As you work to foster transparency, psychological safety, and continuous learning, remember that the goal is not to eradicate organizational hierarchy completely but to ensure that it serves your teams and doesn't stifle them.

In a culture that resists unhealthy hierarchy, employees can truly feel like owners and actively help shape the future of an organization. The journey toward such a culture requires intention and a willingness to challenge the *status quo*, but the reward is a more engaged workforce, innovative ideas, and a shared sense of purpose. That's worth the journey.

Take Action

Resist Hierarchy

Significantly altering your organization's hierarchy may be challenging and depends largely upon your authority. No matter what your role may be, it's possible to take meaningful steps to alter hierarchical decision making within your area of leadership.

Here's a practical way to start:

1. **Identify one decision-making process** in your team or department that is currently centralized.

2. **Schedule a meeting** with your team to discuss this process.

3. **During the meeting**:

   o Explain your desire to decentralize this decision-making process.

- o Ask for input, especially on whether this could be done and how the team thinks this decision could be made at a lower level.
- o Discuss what information or resources would be needed to support this change.

4. **Choose one specific aspect** to decentralize based on the team's discussion.

5. **Implement the change**, ensuring the team has the necessary information and support. Schedule a follow-up meeting one month out to review its impact and make any adjustments needed.

30

The Secret to Collective Ownership: Goal Setting

"Alone we can do so little; together we can do so much."

- HELEN KELLER, author and disability rights advocate

I'm often asked, "How do you inspire a collective sense of ownership on a team? You know, that sense of ownership that makes it OURS and not just one person's MINE?"

There's no simple answer to this question. Many factors contribute to a common sense of ownership within teams. But that said, a linchpin of collective ownership is having a process that involves people in setting team goals. It's even better if many people are involved in setting the organization's goals.

We previously discussed job crafting, which is a method that allows employees to have a direct influence over their individual responsibilities and how they interact with others. Job crafting helps to foster a sense of MINE in ownership, but setting goals collectively is what will help develop that sense of OURS.

Depending on the size of your organization, this can take different forms. For large organizations, collective goal setting will need to be done at group or department levels. For smaller businesses with fewer than 50 people, it may be possible to get almost everyone involved in setting the company's goals for the following year.

COLLECTIVE GOAL SETTING: FROM BOARDROOM TO BREAKROOM

Collective goal setting sounds like a nice idea, but many resist it because they think it's too impractical. How do you translate the ideal of collective goal setting into actual practice—especially within a large organization, where getting everyone involved seems logistically impossible?

The answer lies in adopting a scaled approach to goal setting. While it's true that the effective group size for decision making tends to max out at around six to eight people, this doesn't mean that only the top executives should be involved in setting goals. The process can occur at multiple levels, with each team or department setting its own goals that align with the overall objectives of the organization.

In *The Advantage*, bestselling author Patrick Lencioni describes what he calls the "Cascade of Clarity," a process whereby strategic goals set at the top cascade down through the organization.[87] This begins with the executive team setting broad strategic objectives. These are then communicated to the next level of leaders, who translate the high-level goals into more specific objectives relevant to their area of the business. This process continues down throughout the organization, allowing every team and individual to understand how their work contributes to the larger goals.

Communication plays a crucial role in this process. Each level of the organization must clearly understand the goals set by the level above, and leaders at each level must be open to feedback from their teams. If one is not careful, the "cascade" coming from upper levels can make it seem as if company goals are merely being dictated from the top. Of course, in one sense, this

---

[87] Patrick Lencioni, *The Advantage: Why Organizational Health Trumps Everything Else in Business*, 1st ed. (San Francisco: Jossey-Bass, 2012).

is true—but the key is to ensure that lower levels believe they have the ability to influence *how* those goals are achieved. Leaders must also ensure that there is two-way dialogue between levels. Open communication ensures that goals are realistic, relevant, and well understood by everyone.

> "People are no longer just following orders—they're actively contributing to the strategy and direction"

INVOLVEMENT, OWNERSHIP, AND MEASURING SUCCESS

By including employees at all levels in your goal-setting processes, you give people influence over their projects and a sense of ownership in their work. People are no longer just following orders—they're actively contributing to the strategy and direction being pursued by their teams and the larger organization.

But *creating* goals is only one side of the ownership equation. If someone set a weight-loss goal at 30 pounds but never weighed themselves again, this would be great evidence that they had *not* taken ownership of the goal. To truly "own" a goal, a person must track progress and be accountable for the results.

It's crucial, therefore, that everyone be involved in the development of tracking measures and monitoring. Leaders sometimes involve others in goal setting but then forget to include them in developing the key performance indicators (KPIs) that measure progress. Employees must understand the KPIs, why they are relevant, and how they work. This might require some education, especially if sophisticated financial metrics are used.

The purposes of the "Cascade of Clarity" are to establish clear goals for success at each level and to ensure everyone understands how those goals are measured. People must also see how their goals align with the overall strategic objectives. Regular group check-ins will keep progress on track and help everyone maintain the sense that the goals are OURS. Celebrating successes, both big and small, can further reinforce your team's sense of ownership and commitment to the goals they collectively set.

Let's look at an example of how a collective goal-setting process might look in practice.

THE CASCADE OF CLARITY IN PRACTICE

Revstar Solar Industries is a fictional mid-sized company specializing in renewable energy solutions; it wants to implement a collective "Cascade of Clarity" goal-setting process. Here's the approach they took:

1. **Clarity and Transparency at the Top**. The eight-person executive team at Revstar held a two-day offsite meeting to establish overarching goals for the upcoming fiscal year. An experienced external facilitator ran the meeting to ensure productive and focused discussions. The executive team engaged in healthy conflict and debate, ultimately emerging with four clear, achievable, and aligned goals for the next year. These top-level strategic goals were then communicated to all employees during a company-wide meeting and made available on the company's internal website.

2. **Cascading Goal Setting**. To ensure alignment and clarity across the organization, Revstar implemented a cascading goal-setting process. Each department (e.g., Engineering, Sales, Marketing) was tasked with setting departmental goals that aligned with the overarching company goals. The department heads facilitated numerous goal-setting workshops with their respective teams, ensuring as many individuals as possible were involved in the process. The departmental goals, once finalized, were shared with the executive team for approval and then distributed to other departments.

3. **Cross-Departmental Collaboration**. To promote a collaborative spirit and avoid the "silo" mentality, Revstar also introduced inter-departmental goal-setting meetings. In these sessions, representatives from each department came together to discuss their goals and how they intersected. This ensured that each department understood the objectives of the other departments and identified areas of collaboration and potential conflict early on. In some cases, these meetings resulted in departments revising their goals for better alignment.

4. **Regular Review and Communication**. To ensure that everyone's goals stayed relevant and were consistently top-of-mind, Revstar implemented a regular review process. Each department held monthly meetings to track progress against their goals, implementing countermeasures and adjusting, as necessary. Department heads met quarterly with the executive team to review progress and discuss any challenges or changes. The CEO also hosted quarterly company-wide meetings to provide updates on overall progress and celebrate achievements.

5. **Reinforcing Clarity**. To further reinforce clarity around the goals, Revstar introduced visual reminders in the workplace. Each department displayed their goals on large boards in their work areas. The company's internal website also prominently featured the overall company goals and progress toward them.

Results. Revstar involved many more employees in the goal-setting process than they ever had in the past. Senior leaders noticed better alignment with the company's top-level objectives and an increased sense of ownership and engagement across the organization. This led to better cross-departmental cooperation and, ultimately, more efficient progress toward meeting annual goals. While it wasn't possible to involve every person in setting the company's overarching goals, cascading the process down through the organization meant everyone's work was noticeably more aligned. Morale and collaboration improved across the board.

The cascading model of collective goal setting can encourage a powerful sense of ownership across an organization. It's also a practical way to include a greater number of team members. By transparently communicating overarching objectives, cascading them into specific departmental goals, promoting cross-departmental collaboration, and continually reviewing progress, an organization can foster the sense of OURS that inspires employees to take collective ownership. No matter where you sit in your organization, you can apply many of the same principles to the teams you lead today.

——————————— For Further Reflection ———————————

1. Think about your organization's current goal-setting process. To what extent does it involve employees at different levels? How might broader involvement impact ownership and engagement?

2. How comfortable are you with the idea of opening the goal-setting process to more people? What challenges or opportunities do you foresee in implementing a more collective approach?

3. Think about the "Cascade of Clarity" concept. How might this approach be adapted or implemented within your specific team or department?

4. Reflect on how goals are currently communicated and tracked in your organization. What changes could make this process more inclusive and foster a greater sense of collective ownership?

Take Action

Collective Goal Setting

After reflecting on these questions, schedule a 30-minute conversation with a colleague in your organization to discuss your thoughts on collective goal setting. Share one idea you have for making your organization's goal-setting process more inclusive. Seek the colleague's perspective on how it might be implemented.

31

How Giving Budget Control Can Supercharge Ownership

"For an employee to take responsibility, they must first be given it."

- Simon Sinek, author of *Start with WHY*

My first job upon graduation from Wake Forest University was as a business analyst with Volvo Commercial Finance in Greensboro, NC. My job was to gather business requirements from users with the goal of translating those requirements for our large internal software teams.

However, there were never any conversations about budget, or how my work could affect it. I really had no idea. Being isolated from the financial side of decision making limited my perceived influence over the project. It likewise curtailed my ability to think strategically or creatively about my recommendations. Ultimately, the lack of budgetary information handicapped my sense of ownership.

When I compare many of my early career experiences (when I had no budgetary authority) to later ones (when I had responsibility for large and small budgets alike), I see an obvious shift in my sense of ownership due to the added task of overseeing a budget. Being responsible for a budget changes an employee's mindset because it helps turn the Key of Influence. It allows them to have influence on an organization's finances in a tangible way.[88] Assigning budget responsibilities is a simple and practical way to cultivate a sense of ownership among your teams.

After all, who typically stresses the most over a company's budget? Business owners, of course. Once someone is entrusted with a budget, no matter how small, they immediately gain a level of influence and autonomy over their projects and are more likely to take on an ownership mindset.

Delegating budget authority is complex. Pushing budgets down into your organization requires that you create a culture of openness around financial matters. You don't just hand over the purse strings and hope for the best; you must foster an environment in which discussing budgets, sharing financial successes and losses, and learning from each other's experiences is not just permitted, but encouraged.

Additionally, it's crucial to ensure that your team has the financial literacy and necessary skills to manage their budgets well. Alongside specific job training—such as mastering the software where your company budget is housed—consider offering broader training sessions, workshops, and mentoring programs to make sure that the people you entrust with budgets understand how the company's financials work and the basics of a profit and loss statement (P&L).

Pushing budgets down into the organization may sometimes require creativity. Take a marketing team, for example. The team can be allocated a budget for their annual promotional campaigns. Each team member could then be entrusted with a slice of that budget for social media advertising, print materials, or event

---

[88] R.M. Kanter, *Men and Women of the Corporation* (New York: Basic Books, 1977); Allan Lee, Sara Willis, and Amy Wei Tian, "Empowering Leadership: A Meta-Analytic Examination of Incremental Contribution, Mediation, and Moderation," *Journal of Organizational Behavior* 39, no. 3 (2018): 306–25, https://doi.org/10.1002/job.2220.

sponsorships. By granting each person control over a part of the budget, the team becomes more accountable for their decisions and is likely to take greater ownership of the project's success. Pushing budgets down to lower levels of the organization also brings greater awareness of both the company's finances and how small decisions impact the entire organization. That type of ownership mindset is what you want to promote.

OTHER PEOPLE'S MONEY

What about the "other people's money" (OPM) problem? How do you motivate someone to manage a budget carefully, as if it were their own, when it's not really their own money? How do you avoid wasteful spending?

This is a real issue faced by many leaders; it is best mitigated through a culture of accountability and transparency. It's also helpful if employee compensation is tied to financial performance (see Appendix, "The Power of Profit Sharing"). When everyone in the organization understands the financial impact of their decisions and sees how their actions contribute to the overall financial health of the company, they are less likely to be wasteful. This is especially true when bonuses are tied to good budget management.

When individuals or teams demonstrate that they've delivered on their objectives within budget (or even under budget), you can make them eligible for some kind of reward. Such rewards don't have to be financial, although they could be.

A FEW THINGS TO WATCH OUT FOR

Budgets are used almost universally in corporate settings, but they are not without their problems.[89] A possible downside to pushing budgets too far down into the organization is that it may lead to an over-emphasis on cost cutting at the expense of innovation. While meeting budget expectations is critical, it's equally important to measure and reward innovation. You therefore might want to establish metrics that also gauge innovation. These could include the number of newly generated ideas, percentage of revenue from new products, or number of successful projects that stemmed from innovative company investments. This encourages employees to focus on both cost efficiency and creative growth.

Another way around this is to allocate a specific portion of the budget exclusively for innovative projects. Google, for example, is well known for doing this. It creates a safe space for experimentation without the pressure of immediate revenue or cost savings.

But beyond metrics, the most crucial way to foster innovation is for your team and company culture to embrace it. Be accessible to discuss and support cutting-edge ideas that might require additional resources or exceed the established budget constraints.

A second possible downside to delegating budgets is the time and resources it takes to maintain them. Employees who are already feeling stretched might see managing a budget as an additional burden instead of a privilege. This is something to discuss with them.

Don't let these downsides stop you from making progress, however. Giving your team members budget responsibilities is

---

[89] M.C. Jensen, "Corporate Budgeting Is Broken—Let's Fix It," *Harvard Business Review* 79, no. 10 (2001): 94–101; Stephen C. Hansen, David T. Otley, and Wim A. Van der Stede, "Practice Developments in Budgeting: An Overview and Research Perspective," *Journal of Management Accounting Research* 15, no. 1 (2003): 95–116, https://doi.org/10.2308/jmar.2003.15.1.95.

a powerful way to lead for ownership. Just remember that you must also support this kind of initiative by creating a culture of transparency, financial literacy, and a shared sense of responsibility for financial losses and successes.

This wraps up the Third Key to unlocking the ownership mindset: Influence.

Take Action

Give Them a Budget

Within the next two weeks:

1. **Identify one area or project** where you could delegate some budgetary responsibility. This could be a small portion of a larger budget or a specific project budget.

2. **Choose a team member** or small group to entrust with this budget. Consider their current role, skills, and readiness for this responsibility.

3. **Schedule a meeting** with the chosen individual(s) to:
   - Explain the budget they'll be responsible for.
   - Discuss the goals and expectations associated with this budget.
   - Address any concerns or questions they might have.

4. **Provide necessary resources**. Ensure they have access to required financial tools or software. Offer basic training on budget management, if needed.

5. **Set up a follow-up meeting**. Schedule a check-in one month after delegating the budget to review progress and address any challenges.

6. **Plan for transparency**. Decide how you'll communicate this budget delegation to the wider team. Consider how to share successes or lessons from this experience.

FOUR KEYS TO OWNERSHIP

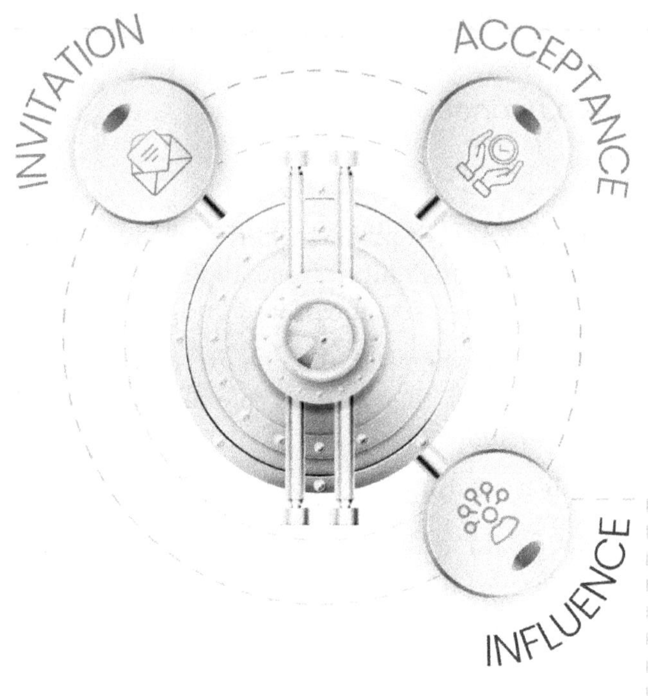

Key #3: Influence

Empower employees to see and feel their genuine
impact on projects

Take Action

- Stop Micromanaging   • Actively Listen   • Connect the Dots
- Job Crafting   • Resist Hierarchy   • Collective Goal Setting   • Give Them a Budget

Section Summary

Key #3: Influence

- Influence is the linchpin of ownership psychology. Without real influence over their projects, employees cannot develop a genuine sense of ownership in their work.

- Common ownership killers include micromanaging, top-down decision making, and failing to listen. These practices undermine employees' senses of agency and discourage ownership thinking.

  o Micromanagement, while often well-intentioned, stifles creativity, undermines trust, and erodes ownership.

  o Leaders must learn to adapt their management style based on each employee's development level.

- Organizational hierarchy often exists in two forms: structural and decision making. The latter, which is often informal, has a more significant impact on employees' sense of ownership.

- Collective goal setting is a powerful tool for fostering shared ownership. Use the Cascade of Clarity to align individual efforts with organizational objectives and give employees a voice in shaping the company's direction.

- Pushing budgetary responsibilities down the organizational hierarchy increases employees' senses of influence and ownership. It connects their day-to-day decisions with the company's financial performance.

KEY #4
INTENTION

32

Key Concept: Why the Future is Vital for Sustained Ownership

"The success of a vision is determined by its ownership by both the leader and the people."

- John C. Maxwell, renowned leadership
coach and bestselling author

The vision you have for your future at a company matters. How do I know? "Short-timer syndrome." I've experienced it, and I bet you have, too. This so-called "syndrome" is a particularly strong form of psychological detachment from work. It usually occurs in earnest after a person has given notice to an employer, but the early stages of short-timer syndrome can begin well before that. When I first started to consider leaving my full-time academic work, I noticed short-timer syndrome beginning to set in. More than once, I had to push myself to stay mentally engaged. It's not unusual. When you start to think that a job or career is "no longer for me," a process of psychological detachment will naturally begin.

Short-timer syndrome is not the only phenomenon relevant to this discussion. In the years following the COVID-19 pandemic, a trend arose called "quiet quitting." Quiet quitting is similar to short-timer's syndrome, but with a twist: employees never hand in their notice. They "quit" their jobs mentally and emotionally, but never actually leave. In 2023, Gallup estimated that almost half of the employees in the United States had quietly quit their jobs.[90]

Quiet quitters lack courage. They stop putting in effort and do only the bare minimum. They don't see a future at their company, but they aren't courageous enough to find something else. Instead, they remain at their organizations and are a drag on everyone's performance.

The Fourth Key of Ownership is all about the psychological mechanisms that create both short-timer syndrome and quiet quitting. When employees no longer intend to stay with your company, their taking psychological ownership becomes almost impossible. That is because, at its core, ownership is a *future-based* psychological state. We take ownership of something in the present, but that ownership requires that we maintain the intention to use or interact with what is owned.

It doesn't matter if you *legally* own something, whether it's a car, a business, or something else. The moment you no longer intend to engage with it, psychologically speaking, you are no longer an owner. You are detached.

People's intentions about the future are often not black or white, so detachment can occur in degrees. Psychological ownership naturally diminishes, little by little, as a person starts to foresee that they won't engage with a project in the future. As we previously discussed, seeing a project as MINE means that a person is attached to, and partially identifies with, the goals of a project.

> "At its core, ownership is a *future-based* psychological state."

In order to maintain this attachment, individuals have to be able to see the project as a part of themselves as they move into

---

[90] Jim Harter, "Is Quiet Quitting Real?," *Gallup Workplace* (blog), May 17, 202AD, https://www.gallup.com/workplace/398306/quiet-quitting-real.aspx.

the future. That's because humans are temporal, future-oriented beings. Our intention of *future involvement* with a project keeps our personal identification and attachment strong. It allows us to "carry" the project with us into the future, so to speak.

A seed of doubt, whether it takes the form of "This group doesn't feel right," "I don't fit in," "I have no future here," or, "I'm contemplating a job change" starts to erode that attachment and identification. At the same time, the sense of ownership also fades.

Empirical studies have shown a positive correlation between psychological ownership and an employee's "intention to stay" with an organization.[91] Without making direct causal claims, these studies suggest that psychological ownership *causes* someone to intend to stay. What I'm arguing, however, is that someone's intention to stay with an organization is best understood as a *necessary condition* for them to maintain a sense of ownership.

So, how well do managers cultivate this intention? It seems that managers and employees have very different perspectives. A 2023 management study found that 85 percent of managers claimed to have had at least one conversation with every direct report about their career vision, but only 52 percent of employees said their manager actually had that conversation. Likewise, 57 percent of managers said their organization offered clear tracks for advancement, but only 36 percent of employees agreed.[92] Having regular career conversations and offering clear tracks for advancement are essential to maintaining an employee's intention to stay. There clearly seems to be room for improvement in this area.

---

[91] Hang Zhu et al., "From Personal Relationship to Psychological Ownership: The Importance of Manager–Owner Relationship Closeness in Family Businesses," *Management and Organization Review* 9, no. 2 (2013): 295–318; Dawkins et al., "Psychological Ownership: A Review and Research Agenda."

[92] 15Five, "Manager Effectiveness Report," Research Report (15five Inc., 2023), https://www.15five.com/2023-manager-effectiveness-report/.

To unlock Intention, the Fourth Key of Ownership, it is vital that you help employees visualize their future at your company. In the following chapters, we'll discuss leadership practices that can help your employees envision a great future at your organization. These include having personal development conversations, maintaining systems of career pathing, and holding stay interviews. Incorporating each of these strategies will significantly improve the culture of ownership within your teams.

———————————— For Further Reflection ————————————

1. Think about a time when you experienced "short-timer syndrome" or witnessed it in others. How did it affect overall team dynamics and the individual's sense of ownership?

2. Consider the relationship between a person's intention to stay at their company and psychological ownership. How might this insight change your approach to fostering ownership among your team members?

3. Reflect on the discrepancy between managers' and employees' perceptions of career conversations and advancement opportunities. How might this gap exist in your organization, and what steps could you take to address it?

33

The Secret to Developing People for Long-term Ownership

"An investment in knowledge pays the best interest."

- Benjamin Franklin, United States
statesman, author, and inventor.

The 2023 study of manager effectiveness conducted by performance management company 15Five Inc. showed that 48 percent of employees report never having had a single conversation with their managers about career development.[93] This statistic is both bizarre and alarming. It seems there is an immense need for managers to develop the habit of holding regular and intentional, one-on-one dialogues focused on career growth and advancement.

Although talent development programs and publicized career tracks have much to be recommended, let me tell you a secret: nothing can replace one-on-one development conversations between you and your team members. That's true for every leader — and if you're a senior leader, it's your responsibility to ensure these conversations are happening at every level within your organization. It's these conversations that will most profoundly shape an employee's perception of their future.

---

[93] 15Five.

What makes for a good development conversation? Beyond discussing how a person may progress through job titles, a good career conversation involves empathy for where an employee is at and where they would like to go, both personally and professionally. When people perceive that you are really interested in their personal growth and development, they are more likely to feel valued. This, in turn, encourages them to envision a longer-term future at your company, releasing them to invest themselves more fully and deeply into their work.

Whatever you do, don't save these discussions for annual performance reviews. Instead, develop a habit of making them a regular part of your interactions throughout the year. These aren't supposed to be formal—they should feel more like brainstorming sessions at a favorite coffee shop, designed to help employees get where they want to be.

BEYOND THE CONVERSATION

Having informal career conversations is the first step toward helping your people catch a vision for their career that makes them want to stay. Here are a few other ways to encourage growth and development that will complement those conversations:

Encouraging Skill Development. Leaders can help individuals recognize the precise skills and knowledge needed for advancement. By proactively providing access to resources like training courses, workshops, and mentoring relationships, you show that you not only care about their ability to do their job today, but also that you want to prepare them for advanced roles within the company tomorrow. Part of leading for ownership is to help your people build their capacity.

Creating Opportunities for Growth. Offer stretch assignments, leadership roles, special projects, and lateral moves that stimulate growth. If you send someone to training, enable the practical application of those new skills in different contexts afterward. These opportunities allow people to apply what they've learned, gain confidence, and demonstrate their capabilities.

Positive Reinforcement. A basic tenet of building new skills is positive reinforcement for work well done.[94] It's not rocket science, but it's astonishingly easy to forget when managers are stretched thin. Recognition and positive feedback are essential for reinforcing an employee's sense of competence. People want to do work well. And they want to belong. When leaders regularly acknowledge a person's progress and accomplishments, this naturally increases their confidence and sense of belonging. Together, these feelings increase their intentions to stay—and the likelihood they'll take ownership.[95]

By showing employees that you value their growth and that they have a good future at your company, you can help cultivate a sense of ownership that benefits both the individual and the organization.

---

[94] James Clear, *Atomic Habits: Tiny Changes, Remarkable Results: An Easy & Proven Way to Build Good Habits & Break Bad Ones* (New York, New York: Avery, an imprint of Penguin Random House, 2018).

[95] Knapp, Smith, and Sprinkle, "Clarifying the Relational Ties of Organizational Belonging: Understanding the Roles of Perceived Insider Status, Psychological Ownership, and Organizational Identification."

────────────── **Take Action** ──────────────

Have Development Conversations

1. **Conduct a team audit**. List all your team members on a sheet of paper. Note the date of your last personal development conversation with each person. Jot down key points you remember from these conversations, including their career aspirations.

2. **Plan your conversations**. Create calendar invites to meet with each team member over the next three to four months. Prioritize those with whom you haven't had any career conversations, and then work backwards, starting with the employees you haven't spoken with in the longest time

3. **Prepare and engage**. Before each meeting, review your notes and think about potential growth opportunities. During the conversation, be fully present and genuinely interested in their aspirations. Listen actively and explore how their goals align with organizational opportunities.

4. **Follow up**. After each meeting, update your audit sheet with new insights. Set reminders to check in on their progress and any agreed-upon actions.

34

How to Reinforce Ownership by Mapping Career Paths

"You cannot predict the future, but you can create it."

- PETER DRUCKER, author and management expert

As part of my on-site ownership workshops, I sometimes run an exercise where leaders prioritize the most important ownership practices they want to develop. They share them, and then try to reach consensus about which practices would improve their company's culture the most. I am always surprised that career pathing seems to consistently be one of the top three items on these lists.

In particular, I'll never forget the leader of a local bank. He stood in front of the group and passionately explained how his mentors had done a good job of vision-casting a future for him at the organization. He gave them credit for helping him find the courage, persistence, and inspiration he needed to rise from being an entry-level bank teller to running an entire branch.

Building the habit of creating clear, meaningful career paths for your employees is essential if you want them to develop a long-term vision of working for your company and to have a strong intention to stay.[96] Career pathing can take various forms, from standardized progression "routes" in larger and more structured organizations to customized career trajectories in businesses where a one-size-fits-all approach isn't feasible.

When you can offer standardized career paths, they provide people clear progression milestones based on acquired skills, training, and experience. This model works well in organizations that have well-defined roles and responsibilities and where people can follow a predictable hierarchy.

Advancement within a standardized career path doesn't necessarily need to involve a change in one's role. Sometimes, advancement can mean assuming increased responsibility, earning a new title, or receiving higher pay for similar work.

In smaller organizations, where roles are more fluid and structure less hierarchical, crafting standardized career paths may not be a viable option. In such cases, leaders can create customized potential career paths for each employee. This requires individualized discussions where you understand an employee's desired career aspirations, and then you collaboratively chart a preliminary trajectory within the organization. As opposed to the informal personal development conversations we discussed in the last chapter, the results of these conversations should be written down.

A customized career path can provide employees with a unique vision for their future growth, including potential timelines and the skills they may need to acquire along the way. This personalized approach not only allows for a higher degree of

---

[96] Kristin M. Schnatter, Jason J. Dahling, and Samantha L. Chau, "Examining Career Pathing Through the Lens of Identity Theories," in *Identity as a Foundation for Human Resource Development*, 1st ed. (Routledge, 2018), 53–65, https://doi.org/10.4324/9781315671482-4.

flexibility, but it also gives employees a stronger sense of agency and investment in their career progression.

Whether a career path is standard or customized, it's crucial that you communicate these potential paths clearly and transparently with employees. People should understand the expectations associated with each step, the skills and experience required, and the evaluation process. This clarity helps people see how they can grow within the organization and whether they are on the right track. It also increases their intention to stay.

Finally, career pathing should be an ongoing conversation, not a one-time event. Regular check-ins with employees to discuss progress, future aspirations, and any necessary adjustments to their career paths are essential. These discussions keep employees engaged and reinforce their connection to the organization's future. As a best practice, you want to have these conversations at least every six months, especially for ambitious or high-performing employees.

BE POSITIVE, BUT FULL OF INTEGRITY

Helping employees envision their careers at your company can be a fun and rewarding activity for leaders. But it must be done with integrity. Being "real" with employees about the limits to their career growth can make these conversations sometimes feel uncomfortable. There will be times when a mismatch exists between an employee's hopes or expectations for their career and what is actually available at your organization. That gap could be a lack of fit—in terms of their capacity, personality, or strengths—or because your company is limited in terms of roles and responsibilities into which people can grow. In these cases, it's important to be honest with employees, while at the same time remaining upbeat about their future.

If the problem is a lack of senior roles in your organization's structure, this can be an opportunity to help employees become more invested and take greater ownership in your company's success. As your company grows, it's more likely that new opportunities and senior positions will open up.

If the problem lies with the employee, first, express appreciation for their current strengths and emphasize how those are crucial and important for your team. Encourage employees to double down on their strengths and provide them opportunities to do so.

Second, help them once again see the worthwhileness of their work (Key #2). Try to keep the conversation as positive as possible, and help people connect the dots on how their work positively impacts the organization, its customers, and society as a whole. When people see the value of their work and know that it is appreciated, it can mitigate their disappointment in realizing that growth opportunities are limited.

To conclude, the goal of career pathing is to ensure that everyone is aligned with some sort of career path. Providing each person with a clear roadmap for growth within your organization improves their sense of clarity and vision for the future. This reinforces their long-term commitment to the organization and intention to stay, which is necessary for a sense of ownership to flourish.

---------------------------- **Take Action** ----------------------------

Career Pathing

1. **Create a career path draft**. Choose one person in your team or department. On a single sheet of paper, sketch out a potential career progression for this role. Include at least three steps or levels of advancement. For each step, jot down two or three key skills or experiences needed to progress.

2. **Reflect on the exercise**. Consider how this career path aligns with your organization's needs and structure. Think about which team member(s) might benefit from seeing this path.

3. **Schedule a follow-up**. Set a calendar reminder to review and refine this career path draft in two weeks. Plan to discuss it with a relevant team member or HR representative for feedback.

35

Why Stay Interviews Are Crucial for Retaining Top Talent

"People leave their manager[s], not their company."

- MARCUS BUCKINGHAM, CO-AUTHOR
of *FIRST, Break All the Rules*

Today was my colleague John's last day. After packing his belongings into boxes and clearing his desk, he walked into my office with a smug look and a slight smirk on his face.

"What are you smirking about?" I asked, somewhat jokingly.

"I just had my exit interview with that lady in HR," he said, chuckling. "What a waste of time!"

"Did you tell her why you are leaving, or say anything about the dysfunction in our department?" I asked.

"Oh, hell no!" he replied.

"Why not?"

"For one, I don't think they really care and wouldn't do anything about it, even if I did tell them," he said. "Also, I want to leave on a good note. I'm moving on. Why sour things with anyone before I go?"

I had seen quite a few people leave this organization saying the same thing, and I understood exactly what John meant.

The idea behind exit interviews (interviewing departing employees) is to learn something about why people leave an organization. But there are two problems with exit interviews. One is that it's already too late. People are out the door, and you must now make a costly rehire. The second is that everyone lies. Sure, you might get glimpses of truth or part of the story about what happened, but there's no real incentive for an outgoing employee to tell you anything. It only puts them at risk, and many people want to leave on a positive note. Even if you get an unfiltered version from a truly disgruntled employee, you may be unlikely to trust that advice or take it seriously.

I'm not a big fan of exit interviews, but I am a big fan of stay interviews. It's exactly what it sounds like: a proactive conversation to figure out why your employees choose to stay with your company and what would cause them to consider leaving. It's a great way to gauge employee satisfaction and foster open communication about their intent to stay. Instead of waiting until they quit, you identify potential issues before they escalate into real retention problems.

Before we go into how to facilitate an effective stay interview, it's important for you to understand the framework and purpose of this kind of interview.

First, a stay interview is voluntary and should feel nonthreatening. This is not an interrogation session. You want your employee to feel comfortable and safe when sharing their thoughts and feelings. That means stay interviews should only be done by people who already have a relationship with the employee. Do *not* send someone from HR to conduct a stay interview on behalf of you or your teams!

Second, a stay interview is about listening. As the "interviewer," your primary role is to listen, understand, and empathize. If you skipped over Chapter 26 on the topic of *active listening,* go back and re-read that chapter. The goal of this conversation isn't to solve a problem. It's to understand current and potential issues. Go in with the approach that you're seeking *only* to understand and validate their experience by reflecting back to the person what you hear. Be open and prepared to receive positive and negative feedback. It's easy to get a little defensive about what might be going wrong on your team, or even with your own leadership style, so make sure you are ready to just listen, smile, and empathize with what you hear. This is *not* the time to start offering explanations, justifications, or excuses.

Third, a stay interview is about taking a proactive approach. Stay interviews are about discovering issues before they become problems, not a last-ditch effort to prevent an employee from leaving. If you already know an employee is unhappy and ready to leave, by all means, you can still talk to them. But just know that the conversation won't be a "stay interview" in the sense we're talking about—i.e. it very likely won't be as relaxed as a stay interview is supposed to be.

CONDUCTING THE INTERVIEW

Let's look at how to conduct an effective stay interview. The guidance I provide here draws from the work of retention expert Richard Finnegan, author of *The Stay Interview: A Manager's Guide to Keeping the Best and Brightest*, along with best practices from HR experts and researchers who study employee retention.[97]

1. **Find a Comfortable Setting.** Set the stage for a truly open and honest conversation. Instead of pulling employees into a formal conference room or office, which often feels intimidating, pick a setting that's more relaxed. Try a cozy corner in the office lobby, a quiet cafe nearby, or even a virtual coffee chat, if you work remotely. Remember, this is—and should *feel like*—a friendly chat. Assure your employee that the conversation will remain confidential, and of course, you have to keep it that way.

---

[97] Richard Finnegan, *The Stay Interview: A Manager's Guide to Keeping the Best and Brightest*, 1st ed. (Nashville: AMACOM, 2015).

Let them know the purpose of the chat when you schedule the meeting, but don't call it a "stay interview" in the invite. You don't want them to show up anxious. Just tell them you want to check in with how work is going to see if there's anything you can do to make it better.

2. **Explain the Purpose**. Start the discussion by explaining the purpose of the stay interview. You might say something like, "I really value your contributions to our team, and I want to understand how we can make your experience working here even better." Or, you might keep it even lighter and add a little humor: "Hey, thanks for your willingness to chat. Don't worry, we're not plotting a corporate takeover here. I just want to better understand what keeps you at the company and what might lure you away…besides a lottery win, of course."

3. **Ask Open-Ended Questions**. Avoid questions with simple "yes" or "no" answers. Open-ended questions invite employees to share more about their experiences. Questions could include:

    "What do you look forward to when you come to work each day?"

    "What might tempt you to leave?"

    "What can we do to make your job more satisfying?"

    These types of questions encourage dialogue and allow you to achieve deeper insights.

4. **Listen Actively and Empathetically**. I'm repeating myself, but this is crucial—the stay interview is a *listening exercise*. Nod, repeat what you hear, and ask follow-up questions, but whatever you do, avoid the urge to multitask or let your thoughts drift elsewhere. Your ability (or inability) to show genuine interest during your conversation will be apparent through the many microexpressions and nonverbal forms of feedback that you inevitably show.

5. **Discuss and Plan Next Steps.** When the interview wraps up, don't leave things hanging like a movie cliffhanger. If your employee raises issues or suggestions, discuss possible next steps, right then and there. You might not know how to solve everything, but take notes. You want the employee to leave the meeting knowing that they were heard, and that their experience is important, whether or not you are ultimately able to fix the issues. You must be committed to making an actual effort to improve the work experience. One of the top ownership killers is soliciting feedback and doing nothing about it. Don't do that! Take action.

After a stay interview, you must follow up—and follow up again. It's essential that you try to address at least one or two of the takeaway issues from the conversation.

If your employee already feels frustrated, they probably believe that nothing will ever change for them. If you hold a stay interview and do nothing afterward, you only confirm that suspicion. Show that you're serious about making changes and want to keep them around. Consider doing the job crafting exercise (See Chapter 28) as a next step. Following up also helps keep the lines of communication open for future discussions.

In summary, stay interviews can be a great way to identify and resolve issues before they lead to turnover. By eliminating obstacles that prevent people from seeing a long-term future at your company, you create a culture where ownership can flourish. In medicine, prevention is better than cure, and this is also true when it comes to retaining your best talent.

Conduct Stay Interviews

Within the next week:

1. **Identify a candidate.** Choose one team member with whom you'd like to conduct a stay interview. Ideally, select someone who's been with the company for at least a year and is a valuable contributor.

2. **Schedule the conversation.** Reach out to the chosen employee and schedule a 30-minute "casual chat" about their experience at the company. Choose a comfortable, informal setting (e.g., a coffee shop or a comfortable area in the office).

3. **Prepare questions.** Write down three to five open-ended questions you'd like to ask, such as:

   o "What aspects of your job do you enjoy the most?"
   o "What would make your work experience even better?"
   o "What keeps you working here?"

4. **Conduct the stay interview.** Start by explaining the purpose of the conversation. Ask your prepared questions and practice active listening. Take mental notes (or written ones) about their responses.

5. **Follow up.** Within 48 hours of the interview, send an email thanking the employee. Include one specific action you plan to take based on their feedback. Set a reminder to meet with the employee in a month for a progress check.

FOUR KEYS TO OWNERSHIP

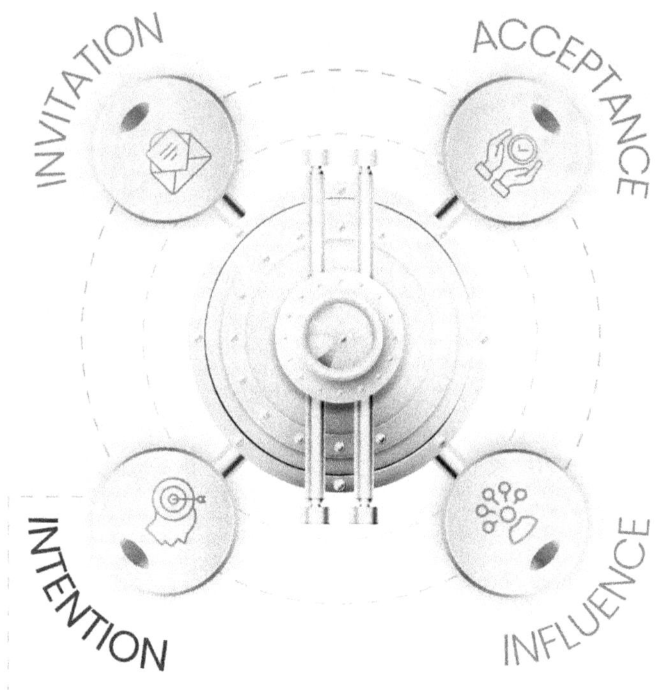

Key #4: Intention

Fostering employees' long-term commitment to the organization

---

Take Action

• Have Development Convos • Career Pathing • Stay Interviews

Section Summary

Key #4: Intention

- Intention to stay is a critical, often overlooked component of psychological ownership. Employees must see a future for themselves in the organization to maintain a sense of ownership in their work.

- Trends like "short-timer syndrome" and "quiet quitting" reflect employees' diminished intention to stay. These trends highlight how leaders must nurture a long-term commitment if their employees are to maintain their sense of ownership.

- Regular, meaningful career development conversations are essential for fostering an intention to stay. These discussions should go beyond annual reviews and focus on personal growth and advancement opportunities.

- Career pathing, whether standardized or customized, helps employees envision their future within the organization. It provides a roadmap for growth and reinforces their long-term commitment, leading to an increased sense of ownership.

- Stay interviews are a proactive tool for addressing employee satisfaction and identifying potential issues before they lead to turnover. They demonstrate an organization's commitment to employee well-being and long-term success.

- Personal development opportunities, clear career progression, and open communication all contribute to strengthening employees' intentions to stay. They create an environment where employees can see themselves growing and thriving in the long term and then feel freedom to fully "own" their projects.

CONCLUSION

36

How to Hire for Ownership and Build Your Team of Owners

"Shaping your culture is more than half done when you hire your team."

- Jessica Herrin, CEO and founder of Stella & Dot

We've covered a lot of ground in this book. We've explored the *Four Keys to Ownership*. We took a deep dive into the psychology of ownership and learned how you can inspire an ownership mindset on your team. But here's the thing: all your efforts to cultivate ownership within your existing team won't mean much if you don't *also* think about ownership when you bring new people on board.

That's why it's important to briefly discuss hiring and firing for ownership before we conclude. It's like putting one last piece of the puzzle in place. When you hire people who are primed for ownership and are also willing to make tough calls on those who resist it, you're setting yourself up for long-term success. After all, creating a culture of ownership isn't just about developing your current team—it's also about shaping the future of your organization through every personnel decision you make.

Let's discuss how to spot potential owners in the hiring process and what to do when someone just isn't cutting it in the ownership department.

My former colleague Barry is the CEO of a mid-sized test and measurement business that has ownership as a company core value. His motto is, "Think like an owner. Act like an owner," and everyone who works for him knows it. During my interviews with Barry, the topics of hiring and firing came up.

"When it comes to my core leadership team, getting the right people on and off the bus quickly is a priority," he told me. "I've made the mistake of trying to coach people [for ownership] for too long, and I've regretted it."

Barry is not a founder-CEO, but someone hired to help grow the company after it was acquired by new investors. He inherited a long-tenured team and chose to make several strategic hiring and firing decisions within his first 12 months. Getting his leadership team right, he told me, was key to the company's cultural transformation.

There's a lot we can learn from Barry's experience. As you know, I believe that every human being is naturally born to take ownership in their work, and the job of a good leader is to bring out this potential. I stand by these claims. It's wrong to assume that ownership is a personality trait and automatically dismiss people as so-called "bad apples." It's right to first examine yourself (and your organization) for faulty performance. Poor management and company culture can turn any apple bad.

It's also true, however, that some people are conditioned for so long *not* to take ownership that they can be hard to rehabilitate. Learned helplessness and victim mindsets are real things. Some people on your team may—eventually—need to go. You can't turn around the culture of an organization or your department alone; you need other people who are committed to embodying ownership and leading for ownership in order to transform your organization. Sometimes you can make converts. Other times, you'll need to hire allies from the outside.

Leaders must make judgment calls about how long they're willing to wait to see changes in behavior after inviting others to take ownership (Key #1) and attempting to turn the remaining Keys. Barry's advice about hiring and firing seems wise, especially for senior leaders. Sometimes, people have to go. There are trade-offs and opportunity costs involved in coaching others for too long or waiting for them to change, especially when they are part of your senior leadership team.

As a helpful rule of thumb, then, we can say that senior leaders should expect more—in terms of changed mindsets and behaviors—from those immediately reporting to them and those people further down in the organization. It seems wise to expect more from your core team and be more patient with those who are less senior. These are judgment calls, though, and are always more of an art than a science.

Let's turn to hiring next.

You can find a plethora of resources providing the best practices for how to interview and hire potential job candidates. I'm not going to recapitulate those ideas here. You are also likely going to be seeking out specific capabilities, skills and character traits. Since ownership is likely only one of these, what follows is not meant to be comprehensive hiring advice. There are, however, two practices for you to consider as you include "ownership" in your hiring process.

First, ask behavioral questions that focus directly on ownership during interviews. If you are hiring for an individual contributor role, you can ask specific questions about how someone took ownership within projects in past roles. Pose questions that allow you to see evidence of the "expressions of ownership" that we discussed in Chapter 4, including a prospective hire's motivations, emotions, and actions. Follow up on the answers to dive deeper, as needed.

Also, listen for whether people have a shared sense of ownership (OURS) when they describe past projects. Try to find people who do not err by taking "extreme" ownership or claiming projects only as MINE.

A simple technique you may want to try during the interview itself is to make a soft invitation to ownership, right then and there. Explain the importance of taking ownership as an ingredient to succeeding at your company and what that looks like in the role you're hiring for, then see how they respond. You'll probably learn a lot.

When hiring for a leadership role, ask questions that reveal how well a leader embodies the various practices and habits of ownership we discussed throughout the book. Probe using each of the Four Keys, asking the candidate specific questions about how they led others in terms of inviting ownership, gaining acceptance, giving influence, and helping make it so people want to stay at past organizations. Ensure that they show at least some competency in all four Keys.

The second important factor in hiring for ownership concerns your onboarding process. The truth is, you only get to onboard a person once, and they only get one first impression of your company. Presumably you've made a great hire, but now is not the time to take your eye off the ball and let that person have a bad first experience. Besides all the typical stuff—having their computer, business cards, and calendar invitations for meetings during their first few weeks ready—a great onboarding should include elements of all Four Keys.

Invite them to ownership right away. Take time to orient new hires to your company values and cast a vision for the good your company does. Make sure they understand the worthwhileness of your collective work. Give each person the ability to have a real influence in the first projects you first assign them, and don't wait too long before having those initial development conversations.

This isn't comprehensive advice. But by becoming more aware and intentional about interviewing for ownership and onboarding your team, you are sure to make better hires and sustain your culture of ownership in the long term.

In the next chapter, we'll put it all together and discuss where you go from here.

Take Action

Hire for Ownership

1. Reflect on your current hiring process. How well does it assess candidates for an ownership mindset?

2. Visit www.ownershipunlocked.com/interview to access our curated list of interview questions designed to probe for ownership potential in candidates.

3. Choose several questions from the list that resonate most with your organization's culture and hiring needs and incorporate these questions into your next hiring interview.

4. After the interview, evaluate how effectively these questions helped you assess the candidate's ownership mindset. Modify questions for the next candidate, as needed.

37

The Ultimate Guide to Put the Four Keys into Action

"The way to get started is to quit talking and begin doing."

- WALT DISNEY, founder of The Walt Disney Company

The principles of leading for ownership aren't difficult to understand. But like many things in life, the challenge is getting ourselves to start taking action. This concluding chapter provides ideas about how to begin incorporating these principles into your day-to-day life so you can begin reducing stress, improving team effectiveness, and creating space for yourself to work on the things that you enjoy.

The sheer number of leadership practices we've discussed might feel daunting, but please, don't let the numbers overwhelm you. These are just different practical ways to put into practice the four principles of psychological ownership. You can make significant progress with your team by implementing even a few of them. As you may recall from Chapter 9, the mere act of inviting your employees to take ownership can significantly alter their performance.

Hopefully you've taken action along the way, as I've provided quick action steps at the end of each chapter. As a reminder, you can download these exercises, along with reflection questions, as a part of the Reflection and Quick Action Guide at www.ownershipunlocked.com/guide.

For review, the table below contains short descriptions of the leadership practices we discussed, associated with each key.

Table 37.1

Ownership Key	Leadership Practice
Key #1: Invitation	• Offer Ownership in One-on-Ones • Stop Giving Answers (a.k.a. 3 Coaching Questions) • Make Job Responsibilities Explicit • Recognize Their Efforts • Plan Collaboratively
Key #2: Acceptance	• Develop & Share Your Why • Departmental Mission Statement • Reframe the Work • Share Testimonials • Develop a Core Credo
Key #3: Influence	• Stop Micromanaging • Actively Listen • Connect the Dots (Impact Map) • Job Crafting • Resist Hierarchy • Collective Goal Setting • Give Them a Budget
Key #3: Intention	• Personal Development • Career Pathing • Stay Interviews

As a place to start, I suggest choosing one practice from each of the Four Keys that you commit to implementing in the next 30 days. This can improve the sense of ownership on your team quickly. You can then add other leadership practices to your repertoire over time.

I advise clients to take a two-pronged approach when considering which practices to choose. This approach involves conducting a team audit and reflective self-assessment. (I'll explain them both shortly.) These steps are easy to do and don't require anything but a pencil and paper. Together, the team audit and the self-assessment will help you select leadership practices to work on because they approach the same issues from different angles. They give a picture of where you can focus your energies, and on whom, so that you can get the biggest results quickly and in the most effective way.

Let's begin with the team audit. Every team is a unique blend of people, personalities, roles, and responsibilities. A great way to begin thinking about how to instill more ownership in your team is to understand the current situation for each individual.

I suggest taking out a piece of paper (in landscape orientation) and listing each person's name along the left-hand side. You'll need to leave a couple inches between each name so that you have a place to write. If you have a large team, that means you'll need more than one piece of paper.

Then, make five columns to the right. At the top of the first column, write "Degree of Ownership." Under this heading, you will rate each team member on your perception of their degree of ownership: Are they detached from work? Are they over-invested? Or somewhere in the middle? Draw a little scale such as the one depicted below and make a dot where you see them on the scale. Note why you gave them this rating.

Figure 37.1

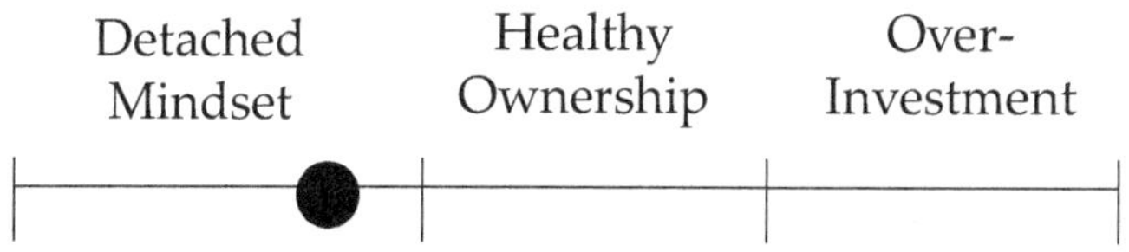

For the remaining four columns, add headings with the names of the Four Keys: "Invitation," "Acceptance," "Influence," and "Intention" (or "Intention to Stay").

As you look at each person's name, consider whether or not Keys have been turned (or still need more turning) for that employee. Try to take *their* perspective, not your own. Do you think they feel like they are consistently invited to take ownership in their work (Invitation)? Do you think they have a good vision for how their work (and your company) makes the world better (Acceptance)? How do you assess their perception of the influence they have on their projects (Influence)? And finally, what do you think their view is toward their future at your company (Intention to Stay)?

For each answer, make note of any evidence for your answers, then give each person a ranking between one (low) and five (high) for each Key in the respective column. One means you don't think that Key is being turned well; five means you think things are going very well. Finally, tally up the scores and write the sums in the first column, next to how you described their degree of ownership. If you find this hard to visualize, you can download a free worksheet at https://www.ownershipunlocked.com/worksheet.

When you're done, you'll have an overview of your team and can immediately see who is better off, and worse off, in terms of how you perceive their ownership. You probably want to focus your efforts first on team members who seem detached and have the lowest scores. You might also notice patterns within the Keys as you glance across the page(s). Patterns often emerge in terms of which Key seems to be doing well across your entire team, and which Key (or Keys) need more work. Those patterns often reflect our own leadership style, which is why you will do a self-assessment next.

After you've completed your team audit, you're ready to evaluate your leadership across the four Keys. Leadership begins by setting an example, so it's important that you consider how you take ownership before asking others to do so. For this exercise, create a similar sheet with five columns for yourself. In the first column, reflect on how well you take ownership of your own work. Make notes on what you do well and where you need to improve. Note feelings of detachment or over-investment on specific projects and explore why you may feel this way.

Next, in the four columns to the right, ask yourself whether and how you unlock each Key for the people you lead. For example, in the "Invitation" column, note if and when you had one-on-one conversations specifically about ownership with each of your team members. Also, think about how you react when each person comes to you with problems. Do you take over, or do you invite them to own the issues themselves? (Note: you might not treat everyone the same.) What are the specific ways you acknowledge and recognize people's efforts to take ownership? Which people do you include in determining your group's plans or KPIs?

You can generate these kinds of self-examination questions by reviewing the leadership practices aligned with each Key, using the table above. Alternatively, we have a list of self-examination questions you can download along with the worksheet.

In your review, make notes about the practices you perform well, those that you have incorporated to some extent and could build upon, and those that need improvement. It's important to celebrate what you are doing well, so you are encouraged to continue those practices.

With both completed assessments in hand, the next task is to identify and implement one practice for each Key *in the next 30 days*. That's four habits in 30 days—no more.

But this raises a few questions. With so many practices, how am I supposed to pick? What if I need improvement in a lot of areas? How should I choose which ones to work on first?

I suggest you look both at your own self-assessment and the audit you did for the team. Compare them: where do they overlap? Which habits that you want to develop personally can also have the biggest impact on your team? There are no right or wrong answers. Pick leadership habits and practices that excite you and will provide the greatest benefit for your team.

However, if you get stuck, here are four practices you can't go wrong with:

Practice for Key #1: Invite Ownership in One-on-Ones. This is an essential practice and a great place for everyone to start (see Chapter 10).

Practice for Key #2: Reframe the Work. Even if you haven't got your WHY or Core Credo articulated in clear and definitive statements yet, you can figure out how to reframe everyone's work according to its worthwhileness. This framing will give you a head start on all the other practices that make tangible the Key of Acceptance (see Chapter 17).

Practice for Key #3: Job Crafting. You won't be able to do this with everyone in 30 days, but practice going through the job crafting exercise (see Chapter 28) with at least one team member. You might want to pick whoever has the lowest score. Job crafting gives immediate and tangible influence to employees over their work.

Practice for Key #4: Personal Development. Conduct the personal development audit described at the end of Chapter 33 and then have at least one personal development conversation with a team member.

You'll eventually want to incorporate as many of these leadership practices into the way you lead as you can—which is actually easier than you might think. Many of these practices do not require daily actions. They all involve consistent behavior, but that sometimes means you just need to plan or schedule them out. It's also okay to be transparent with your team about your desire to grow as a leader, and that you're going to be working on these things over time. Your leadership journey is a collaborative process. Transparency and openness to your team's feedback are essential.[98]

I know that some of you will struggle to complete the team audit because you don't know that much about your team. You might not know whether individuals feel invited to take ownership, whether they understand the good of their work, how they perceive their sense of influence, or even whether they intend to stay at your company. If that describes you, don't worry. Just fill out your audit and make the best guesses you can for now, then make it a point to have conversations with each team member to assess where things really stand. Putting this book's lessons into practice is all part of your growth as a leader.

> "Leading for ownership will positively change the direction of your company and your career."

Now, let's address those in more senior roles—individuals who lead other leaders and manage other managers. The task is similar, but with multiple layers. To affect downstream change within your organization, you need to think through *both* how you increase the sense of ownership in those who report directly to you *and* how you can educate and inspire them to do the same with the people who report directly to them.

Start by auditing yourself and your immediate direct reports, as previously described. Then, to drive the sense of ownership deeper within your organization—which is where much of the

---

[98] For more on the importance of vulnerability and transparency in leadership, see: Brené Brown, *Dare to Lead: Brave Work. Tough Conversations. Whole Hearts.* (New York: Random House, 2018).

work is really being done—you need to work through your team. That means educating them about ownership and holding them accountable.

To do this, you could study this book together over a series of weeks, or you could kickstart your education with a day-long workshop (www.ownershipacademy.com/workshops). We also have online masterclasses and learning communities at the Ownership Academy (www.ownershipacademy.com), where managers can participate with managers from other companies, or exclusively within your organization.

Regardless of how you approach building ownership in your organization, remember: everything starts with the invitation. No progress will be made without communicating your desire that others start taking ownership in their work, and then inviting them to do so. Also remember: you need to turn all *Four Keys to Ownership* at some level if employees are going to retain a long-term sense of ownership. Stifling any one of the Keys can quickly kill a person's sense of ownership. A balanced approach to leading for ownership results in the best outcomes.

Leading for ownership will positively change the direction of your company and your career. It is also one of the best ways to love people, because it empowers and inspires them to do their greatest work. Giving your people a true sense of ownership is one of the greatest gifts you can give them. When you inspire ownership, you are empowering lives and giving everyone a chance to succeed together.

Take Action

Conduct Your Assessment

Download the free worksheet to conduct your team
audit and reflective self-assessment at:
http://www.ownershipunlocked.com/worksheet

OR, we've created a FREE Quiz that can help you
assess where you should focus your efforts.

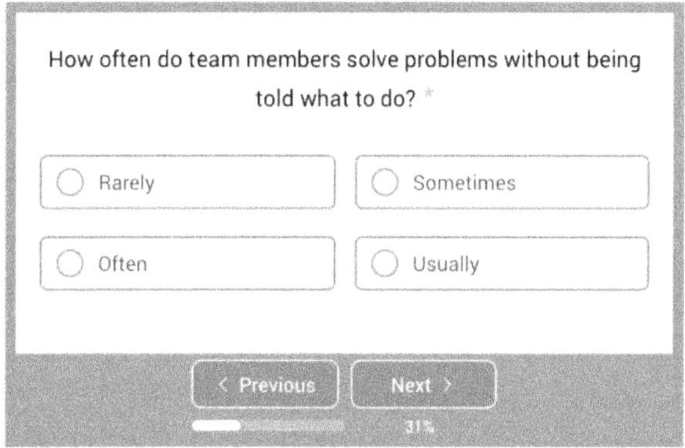

Find out where your biggest opportunities lie!

OwnershipUnlocked.com/Quiz

APPENDIX: FOR BUSINESS OWNERS

APPENDIX

"Culture does not change because we desire to change it. Culture changes when the organization is transformed; the culture reflects the realities of people working together every day."

— Frances Hesselbein, former CEO
of Girl Scouts of the USA

OWNERSHIP FROM THE TOP

It's important to recognize that if an ownership culture isn't supported at the top of an organization, the transformation that others can make will be limited. Some business owners get interested in the idea of ownership, but they expect people below them to make it happen. You as the owner, however, must set the cultural tone through what you say and how people are rewarded.

Company culture starts at the top, and there are certain initiatives that only business owners can make happen. That's why this section exists.

Business owners can employ several organizational strategies to catalyze the efforts of other leaders and help everyone adopt an ownership mindset. These strategies include: (i) adding ownership to your company's core values, (ii) creating profit sharing plans, and (iii) offering equity incentive plans.

Chapter 38 discusses making ownership one of your company's core values. This turns Key #1 of Invitation and broadcasts an invitation to ownership to your entire organization.

Chapter 39 discusses the role that profit-sharing plans can play in creating an ownership culture. Instituting a profit-sharing plan helps to turn Key #3 of Influence because it helps people see the effect of their work (i.e., its influence) in the form of a tangible, financial result. It also focuses employees on the financial performance of the business, which is an important part of thinking like an owner. In this chapter, we discuss some pitfalls to avoid when setting up profit-sharing plans, which can actually hurt ownership instead of helping it.

Finally, Chapter 40 discusses equity incentive plans. These also help to turn Key #3 of Influence, but in addition, they also help to turn Key #4 of Intention. In terms of Influence, they have a similar effect as profit sharing plans. Your employees' efforts and ingenuity directly influence the company's value, and they now share in that value. But while a profit-sharing plan might keep an employee around until the next time bonuses are paid, equity incentive plans can help create a longer-term intention to stay with your company.

Since these strategies are typically only initiated by business owners (or a board of directors) and it would also be a stretch to call them leadership habits or practices, it seemed appropriate to discuss them in a separate section aimed specifically at owners. I'll provide an overview of each strategy and show you how it can impact the culture of ownership you want to build. With the exception of making ownership a company core value, you'll probably want to get more specialized help to implement profit-sharing and equity incentive plans.

38

Making Ownership a Company Core Value

"Ownership: A commitment of the head, heart, and hands to fix the problem and never again affix the blame."

- JOHN G. MILLER, author of *QBQ!: The Question Behind the Question*

InfoTrust is a medium-sized digital analytics company located in Cincinnati, Ohio. It frequently has been celebrated for its award-winning company culture by the likes of *Fortune, Ad Age,* and Inc.'s *Best Places to Work.* Founder and CEO, Alex Yastrebenetsky, leads in a very thoughtful and employee-centric way, with "Take Ownership" as one of the company's core values.

"Because we have a culture that values ownership, I can make a difference within the organization—I am empowered to take initiative—and I can chase down my passions and incorporate that into my position," says Lisa Wilms, Operations and Talent Acquisition Manager. "I feel trusted because the team knows I will do the right thing. We all welcome taking ownership – and because of that, we are absolutely one of the best places to work!"[99]

As I noted earlier, a powerful strategy to encourage ownership is simply to make it one of your company's core values. This

---

[99] Wilms, "What Ownership in the Workplace Means to Me."

functions as an official Invitation to everyone in your company (Key #1) from the top down and emphasizes that you want them to take ownership in their work. Ownership as an official value helps everyone know that taking ownership is important and welcome, and it fits nicely among other common core values like innovation, impact, diversity, growth and respect.

The adoption of ownership as a core value sends a strong message to your teams. Everyone at your company can now feel confident when the topic comes up during one-on-one conversations, promotions, and hiring and firing decisions. It also makes it more likely that taking ownership will be discussed publicly, both in company-wide meetings and between coworkers during breaks. The more people talk about ownership, the more they feel invited to take ownership in the work.

Embracing ownership as a core value can also have a positive effect in stopping or preventing behaviors that undermine ownership, many of which were discussed in the section on Influence. Top-down decision making, micromanaging, and failing to listen are all mitigated to some extent when ownership becomes part of your organization's collective consciousness.

For Further Reflection

1. How might making ownership an explicit core value impact your company's culture?

2. What challenges do you foresee in implementing ownership as a core value across your organization?

3. How could you effectively communicate and reinforce this value to your employees?

39

The Power of Profit Sharing

"No man becomes rich unless he enriches others."

— ANDREW CARNEGIE, American
industrialist and philanthropist

In the 1989 cult classic, *National Lampoon's Christmas Vacation*, Chevy Chase plays Clark Griswold, a middle manager working at a cereal company in Chicago. It's Christmas, and everyone anticipates a holiday bonus.

"Well, the big question is, what are you going to do with that big bonus check?" asks Clark's coworker. "Gonna blow it on yourself, I hope!"

Clark responds somewhat sheepishly. "Me? Heck no."

There's a pause, then Clark slowly pulls out a brochure for a new swimming pool.

"Take a look at this," he says. Then, muttering under his breath, he adds, "I just hope my Christmas bonus check will cover it."

A few days later, when Clark is home with his extended family, the bonus check finally arrives. Before opening it, he announces, "With this bonus check, I'm putting in a swimming pool!"

The room erupts with excitement and joyful shouting. Clark tells everyone that he already wrote a check for the pool, and that without this bonus check, he wouldn't have the money to cover it.

His whole family waits with anticipation as Clark opens the envelope. Everyone falls silent as Clark's face turns into an expression of shock and disappointment.

"How much is it?" someone asks.

Clark replies, "It's a one-year membership to the Jelly of the Month Club."[100]

While fictional, this scene perfectly depicts how a bonus or profit-sharing plan can go wrong. Instead of creating a culture of ownership, the company's profit-sharing plan created an attitude of entitlement—so much so that Clark spent the money before receiving it.

Profit-sharing plans are designed to incentivize employees by giving them a share of the profits, usually on a quarterly or annual basis. This incentive-based form of compensation is also commonly thought to help foster a sense of ownership, and for good reason—everyone has a shared incentive and the power to influence it. People win or lose together, at least financially. However, there are two prevailing misconceptions about profit-sharing plans.

First, it's a myth to think that a profit-sharing plan is necessary to foster a culture of ownership within your teams. As I've maintained throughout the book, psychological ownership is not a product of legal ownership or financial incentive schemes; rather, it's an attachment and an emotional investment to the projects you're working on. People can take ownership in the work of churches and volunteer organizations, endeavors that do not involve any financial incentive.

A second myth is that the act of establishing a profit-sharing plan will, by itself, create an ownership mindset in your employees. When profit-sharing plans work, they allow employees to see how

---

[100] *National Lampoon's Christmas Vacation*, directed by Jeremiah S. Chechik (Burbank, CA: Warner Bros., 1989)

their individual efforts directly influence the financial results of the business. That helps turn Key #3 of Influence. However, profit-sharing plans work only if executed correctly. If mismanaged, they can devolve into entitlement programs and, paradoxically, undermine the very culture of ownership they are designed to promote.

OWNERSHIP OR ENTITLEMENT? POTENTIAL PROFIT-SHARING PITFALLS

In his book *Ownership Thinking,* international consultant Brad Hams presents striking examples of how profit-sharing plans can lead to a culture of entitlement rather than ownership.[101] Just like the scene from *National Lampoon's Christmas Vacation*, this happens when employees start to view profit sharing as a guaranteed perk rather than an earned reward. Instead of promoting a sense of ownership and shared responsibility, profit sharing can lead to complacency.

PRINCIPLES FOR EFFECTIVE PROFIT SHARING

Hams lays out three key principles for establishing an effective profit-sharing plan that navigates clear of entitlement traps: transparency, involvement, and rewarding actual outcomes.

First and foremost, transparency is critical in a profit-sharing plan. Employees need a clear understanding of the plan's mechanics, including how company profits are calculated and the way that particular KPIs and their own contributions affect the end results. This often requires that business owners, who typically keep detailed financial information under wraps, become more transparent. The shift often starts by educating employees

---

[101] Brad Hams, *Ownership Thinking: How to End Entitlement and Create a Culture of Accountability, Purpose, and Profit,* 1st edition (New York: McGraw-Hill, 2012).

about company finances, which is a worthy investment in its own right. Employees participating in the plan should grasp the basic mechanics of the company's P&L and balance sheet, as well as the key drivers of company performance. This clarity connects the dots for employees between their efforts and the company's financial results.

The second principle is involvement. This doesn't mean that employees are responsible for the plan's technical or legal details, but they should have a voice in shaping the plan's structure and function, if possible. This participatory role cultivates a sense of influence and accountability, further reinforcing the ownership mindset. It can be helpful to revisit the plan with a representative group of employees every few years. You want to ensure that the plan actually works and cultivates the sense of ownership it's designed to achieve.

Finally, the third principle is that a profit-sharing plan needs to recognize and reward tangible results, not just effort. This involves linking profit sharing to specific, measurable outcomes that mirror the business's overall success. Upholding this principle ensures that profit sharing is perceived not as a given right but as a merit-based reward for boosting the company's financial performance.

Profit-sharing plans that pay out nebulous lump sums at the end of the year—or those that are not clearly and directly tied to specific performance metrics—end up creating a mindset of entitlement, not ownership. When companies issue the customary "annual Christmas bonus," they may unintentionally dampen the sense of shared responsibility and ownership among employees. Employees begin to see such bonuses as something owed to them. Instead of a genuine incentive, it devolves into an expected holiday gift, kind of like fruitcake.

There is no doubt that a profit-sharing plan can help reinforce your company's culture of ownership. But the plan must be crafted and communicated carefully, and it's important to remember that it is only one tool in your toolbox. Establishing a profit-sharing plan is not a silver bullet. You and other leaders still need to do the hard work of leading for ownership. To be effective, profit sharing must be part of a broader strategy to unlock the ownership mindset across all four Keys.

For Further Reflection

1. How might a profit-sharing plan align with your company's current goals and culture?

2. What potential pitfalls do you see in implementing a profit-sharing plan in your organization?

3. How could you involve employees in the design and implementation of a profit-sharing plan?

4. If you already have a profit-sharing plan, are there steps you could take to ensure its transparency?

40

Aligning Interests Through Equity

"The real risk is doing nothing."

- Denis E. Waitley, author of *The Psychology of Winning*

The summer of 2008 was a big moment: I received stock options at Danaher for the first time. I was so excited. It felt like I had finally made it to the big leagues of the corporate elite, as now I was officially viewed as valuable enough to be granted equity.

But just like the "high" everyone experiences when getting a bonus, a raise, or some other form of compensation, the elation soon faded. Although I was now technically a company "owner," my position was still pretty low on the totem pole. It soon became clear that my motivation to take ownership would not be determined merely because I received some options. It would come down to the daily realities of my job, the interactions I had with my manager, and my ability to influence my team's projects.

The motivating power of equity—*as a form of compensation*—was, for me, marginal at best. Danaher is a multi-billion-dollar conglomerate, and I didn't think I could personally do much to affect the company's stock price or the value of my options.

But receiving the options did shift my mindset toward being an owner in a rather unexpected way. It made me feel valued and recognized, and it helped me see myself as an integral part of the team and my company. This different way of "seeing" mattered much more than the potential dollars. I now saw a future at the company that I hadn't before.

My experience is not unique. A 2013 Rutgers University study of over 40,000 employees in 14 corporations found that granting employee ownership, even at very low thresholds, positively influenced attitudes toward one's job and toward the company.[102]

Entrepreneurs and private business owners often fall into one of two camps in terms of how they view equity incentive plans. On one hand, business owners may issue equity incentives to employees hoping that the financial incentive alone will foster a sense of ownership. They believe that employees who are given a so-called "slice of the pie" should also start thinking and acting like owners. Business owners are often surprised and frustrated when employees who have been issued equity still lack a sense of ownership in their work.

Steve, the former CEO of a publicly traded pharmacy, recalled this experience. Soon after going public, he and his leadership team issued options to every employee, down to the truck drivers. They were very disappointed in the results.

"We learned the hard way you can't just assume giving people the economic incentive of ownership will actually make them take ownership," Steve told me. "[Stock] options programs need to be enveloped by systems and ways of leading that support psychological ownership. We should have established those first, and then issuing options would have been more effective."

Corey Rosen, who has consulted with hundreds of employee-owned companies and is the director for the nonprofit National Center for Employee Ownership (NCEO), agrees, saying, "[Equity]

---

[102] Dan Weltmann, Joseph Blasi, and Douglas Kruse, *At What Threshold Do Employee Shares Have a Meaningful Effect?* (New Brunswick, NJ: Rutgers University School of Management and Labor Relations, 2013).

is a great and important benefit, but not a day-to-day motivator for most people."[103]

Granting equity by itself will not inspire the sense of ownership that so many business owners long for in their people.

On the other hand, some business owners resist issuing equity at all. It takes a lot of courage, hard work, and sweat equity to get a business off the ground, and these owners don't want to give away equity to people who did not take the upfront risk of starting or buying their businesses. It's also true that plenty of great companies have been built without using equity incentives, so it's certainly not necessary for success.

In fact, giving equity to employees is actually not that common. Only about a quarter of private sector employees, or an estimated 26.3 million Americans,[104] hold company stock or stock options as part of their compensation package. With roughly 167.8 million Americans in the workforce (including government workers), that means only about 15 percent of the working population receives company stock.

The real question is, what should you do?

I'm not here to tell you how to allocate your company's stock, but I want you to be informed. Management studies show that equity incentives help to foster a sense of psychological ownership among employees, even among entry-level workers.[105] Research

---

[103] Rosen, *Beyond Engagement*.

[104] Rutgers Institute for the Study of Employee Ownership and Profit Sharing (2023).

[105] Nai-Wen Chi and Tzu-Shian Han, "Exploring the Linkages between Formal Ownership and Psychological Ownership for the Organization: The Mediating Role of Organizational Justice," *Journal of Occupational and Organizational Psychology* 81, no. 4 (2008): 691–711, https://doi.org/10.1348/096317907X262314; Jan C. Hennig et al., "Employee Stock Ownership and Firm Exit Decisions: A Cross-Country Analysis of Rank-and-File Employees," *Accounting, Organizations and Society* 104 (2023): 101390-, https://doi.org/10.1016/j.aos.2022.101390.

also shows that employees with equity are more likely to stay,[106] and their companies generally perform better.[107] As NCEO's Rosen notes, it's easier for someone to care about the value of their company when they participate in the value being created.[108] When employees have skin in the game, it's more likely they will be concerned about a company's performance.[109]

Granting employees equity in your business also helps to create a culture where your people feel valued and like they belong. It creates a shared sense of OURS. It also establishes the fact that you want them around for the long run, which helps bolster their intention to stay. In other words, equity complements many of the psychological drivers of ownership we've discussed throughout the book. Just like profit-sharing plans, granting equity is not a silver bullet. But if you're serious about building a culture of ownership, it's a great catalyst to enable ownership psychology.

The remainder of this chapter briefly presents some options you might consider in structuring an equity-based incentive plan. Some of these equity structures are relatively well-known, such as offering stock options and restricted stock. Others may be less familiar. The list is not meant to be comprehensive, nor is it legal advice. I merely wish to outline some different ways that you might issue equity to the key people in your organization so they can take part in its ownership structure. Some business owners

---

[106] Hennig et al., "Employee Stock Ownership and Firm Exit Decisions."

[107] Joseph Blasi, Richard Freeman, and Douglas Kruse, "Do Broad-Based Employee Ownership, Profit Sharing and Stock Options Help the Best Firms Do Even Better?" *British Journal of Industrial Relations* 54, no. 1 (2016): 55–82, https://doi.org/10.1111/bjir.12135.

[108] Rosen, *Beyond Engagement*, 7.

[109] Part of helping employees care about financial performance involves bringing them into a deeper understanding of your business's financials. This requires education, financial literacy, and financial transparency so they can see how decisions impact the bottom line (see Chapter on Profit Sharing for more discussion).

assume that issuing equity is only for large corporations, but that's not the case.

The proposed plans below may serve to help you begin a conversation with your legal or financial advisor. My hope is to spark your interest and awareness.

TYPES OF EQUITY PLANS

Equity incentive plans can be divided along two different lines. The first depends on whether your company is structured as a corporation or an LLC (Limited Liability Company) that is taxed as a sole proprietorship or a partnership. The second depends on whether you issue employees real equity or what is known as synthetic equity.

Real equity involves the transfer of actual shares or stock options in the company, while synthetic equity mimics the financial features of owning equity without actually conveying ownership in the company. The latter is more complex but is sometimes chosen for non-financial reasons (often tax issues, voting, or other governance issues). The following chart lists some of the most common equity incentive structures.

Table 40.1

	Real Equity	Synthetic Equity
C Corporation	Stock Options, Restricted Stock	Phantom Stock, Stock Appreciation Rights (SARS)
LLC	Profits Interest	Phantom Equity, Stock Appreciation Rights (SARS)

Stock Options (C-Corp, Real Equity). In the case of C-Corporations, stock options are relatively straightforward. They give your employees the right to purchase shares in the company at a set price. This price is typically the fair market value at the time the option is granted. If you are a private company, that means you will need a 409a valuation annually (or whenever your company's value materially changes). This is an estimate of your company's enterprise value and is usually conducted by an outside firm. There are plenty of firms that provide these services, so don't let that intimidate you.

Options issued to employees have a "strike price" that is based on your firm's valuation when they are issued. The strike price is simply the price per share at which employees may purchase stock in the future. Assuming your company becomes more valuable, employees can "exercise" their options and purchase company shares at the lower contracted strike price and sell at a profit. This model aligns an employee's financial interests with the growth and prosperity of the company, and it may be motivating, especially if you intend to sell the business someday.

Restricted Stock (C-Corp, Real Equity). Restricted stock is a form of real equity that involves giving employees shares in the company, but with several restrictions. As with most forms of equity compensation, these shares typically vest over time to incentivize long-term employment.

Phantom Stock or Phantom Equity (C-Corp or LLC, Synthetic Equity). Phantom stock, or phantom equity (in the case of an LLC), provides employees with many of the financial benefits of stock ownership without actually giving them any company stock. This avoids diluting the ownership of existing shareholders. Phantom stock rights grant a future cash bonus equivalent to the value of a certain number of shares or member units. The value of phantom stock rises and falls with the company's actual stock (or estimated value), which provides an equivalent economic benefit to actual stock ownership.

Stock Appreciation Rights (SARs) (C-Corp or LLC, Synthetic Equity). SARs are similar to stock options in that they can provide value if the company's stock price increases. However, SARs differ in that employees receive only the appreciation in value, not the underlying stock itself. Upon exercise, employees receive the monetary equivalent of the increase in the company's stock price between the grant date and the exercise date, multiplied by the number of SARs granted. This can be paid out in cash or stock. SARs can simplify administration and accounting for companies, as they don't involve actual share issuance and can be settled in cash.

Profits Interest (LLC, Real Equity). A profits interest is a type of equity compensation unique to LLCs. It provides the recipient the right to a share of the LLC's future profits and appreciation in value above a specified threshold, typically the LLC's value at the time of grant. Unlike capital interests, which represent a stake in the LLC's current and future value, profits interests only provide rights to future growth, allowing for a unique tax treatment—i.e. they can often be issued without triggering an immediate taxable event for the recipient. These are sophisticated instruments with nuanced tax and legal implications, and their implementation should be handled only with the advice of skilled legal and tax professionals.

Before concluding, let me offer a quick note about vesting. Typically, all forms of equity come with a vesting period, which means that an employee doesn't obtain the right to their equity until certain conditions have been met. At minimum, equity typically vests over a period of three to five years (sometimes as long as 10 years), which is a way to both incentivize long-term employment and make sure you're not giving equity to someone who leaves your company after six months.

However, it's important to be aware that time-based vesting schedules are not the only restrictions that can be placed on equity. Performance-based vesting is another common restriction.

In this case, shares vest only if the employee or the company as a whole reaches certain predefined goals. These goals can be based on individual performance metrics (such as project completion or annual individual sales), company-wide profitability, or achieving fundraising targets or a certain growth rate. The goal can really be any parameter that is important to you. If you can think of it, your legal team can probably craft it into your equity plan.

So, that's it. I hope this high-level overview of the options available has been helpful. Again, it's important to work with a qualified attorney and tax advisor due to differences in tax and legal consequences based on your jurisdiction and the type of plan. It's also worth noting that this area of business and tax law is always changing.

Management research and common sense align on the idea that when people have real ownership in a business, it positively impacts their intention to stay and fosters an ownership mindset. By incorporating equity into your overall compensation plans, you can simultaneously help to turn the *Four Keys to Ownership*.

———————————— For Further Reflection ————————————

1. How might offering equity impact your company's long-term strategy and employee retention?

2. How could you balance the benefits of equity grants with potential dilution of ownership?

3. What steps would you need to take to educate employees about the value and implications of equity ownership?

ABOUT THE AUTHOR

Matthew F. Wilson, Ph.D., is a recognized authority in psychological ownership and transformative leadership. With over two decades of experience in Fortune 500 companies and universities, Matthew has dedicated his career to helping leaders foster ownership within their teams. As the founder of the Ownership Academy, he equips leaders to unlock their team's potential using his innovative "Four Keys to Ownership" framework. Matthew's approach bridges rigorous research with practical application, providing actionable strategies for real-world success. He holds an M.B.A. from Indiana University and a Ph.D. from Baylor University. When he's not writing, speaking, or consulting, Matthew enjoys mountain biking and hiking the trails of Northwest Arkansas with his wife and three children. Learn more at MatthewFWilson.com.

Get In Touch

Hi there!

If you'd like to share feedback on the book or hire me to speak at your company, you can reach me at: <u>mwilson@ownershipacademy.com</u>.

(Yes, that's my real email!)

I also encourage you to join the Ownership Academy for additional training, templates, and resources.

www.ownershipacademy.com

Your Feedback Matters!

Dear Reader,

Thank you for taking the time to read *Ownership Unlocked*. I hope this book has brought you fresh insights, valuable tools, and inspiration on your journey to becoming a more effective leader.

If you found value in these pages, I would be deeply grateful if you could take a moment to leave a review.

Your review not only helps others discover the book but also supports me in continuing to create content that serves you and others like you. It's one of the most meaningful ways you can give back.

It's Simple to Leave a Review—Even if You Didn't Buy the Book on Amazon!

1. Visit the link below or scan the QR code:
   OwnershipUnlocked.com/Review

   (redirects to Amazon page)

2. Follow Amazon's instructions for leaving a review.

   Your feedback can inspire someone else to take ownership of their work and lead with purpose. Thank you for being a part of this community of self-driven leaders!

With appreciation,

Matthew F. Wilson, Ph.D.

WAIT! One More Thing Before You Go....

Imagine the Impact of Your Whole Team Embracing the Principles of Ownership!

If you've found the insights in *Ownership Unlocked* valuable, why not share them with your team or organization? Learning together amplifies the impact and helps create a culture of ownership that drives results.

Special Discounts Available for Bulk Orders!

Equip your team with the tools to take ownership, inspire action, and elevate performance. Purchase multiple copies and enjoy special bulk pricing.

1. **Order 10-24 copies**: 15% off
2. **Order 25-49 copies**: 20% off
3. **Order 50+ copies**: 25% off

To learn more or place an order:

- Visit: **www.OwnershipUnlocked.com/bulkorders**
- Scan the QR code below for quick access

Help your team unlock their full potential with *Ownership Unlocked*. Thank you for spreading the word and building a culture of ownership!

With gratitude,

Matthew F. Wilson, Ph.D.

ACKNOWLEDGMENTS

Many thanks to the people who have been part of the "common project" that helped me bring this book to life:

Daniel McNair, Barry Lyon, Steve Cosler, Jeff Wilson, David Harding, Richard Olson, Pamela Ferdinand, Robert Roberts, C. Stephen Evans, Michael Beaty, Alexander Pruss, James Bruce, Robin Cheriakalth John, Angela Wilson, Tyler VanderWeele, The Society for Business Ethics, Jubilee Centre for Character and Virtues, and the Human Flourishing Program at Harvard University's Institute for Quantitative Social Science.

SOURCES

15Five. "Manager Effectiveness Report." Research Report. 15five Inc., 2023. https://www.15five.com/2023-manager-effectiveness-report/.

Adams, Robert. *A Theory of Virtue*. Oxford: Clarendon Press, 2006.

Anaza, Nwamaka A., and Brian N. Rutherford. "Developing Our Understanding of Patronizing Frontline Employees." *Managing Service Quality* 22, no. 4 (2012): 340–58. https://doi.org/10.1108/09604521211253469.

Aristotle. *Nicomachean Ethics*. Edited and translated by Roger Crisp. New York: Cambridge University Press, 2000.

Ashforth, B. E., and G. E. Kreiner. "'How Can You Do It?': Dirty Work and the Challenge of Constructing a Positive Identity." *The Academy of Management Review* 24, no. 3 (1999): 413–34. https://doi.org/10.5465/AMR.1999.2202129.

Ashforth, Blake E., Spencer H. Harrison, and Kevin G. Corley. "Identification in Organizations: An Examination of Four Fundamental Questions." *Journal of Management* 34, no. 3 (2008): 325–74. https://doi.org/10.1177/0149206308316059.

Avey, James B., Bruce J. Avolio, Craig D. Crossley, and Fred Luthans. "Psychological Ownership: Theoretical Extensions, Measurement and Relation to Work Outcomes." *Journal of Organizational Behavior* 30, no. 2 (2009): 173–91.

Bartunek, J.M. "Rummaging Behind the Scenes of Organizational Change - and Finding Role Transitions, Illness, and Physical Space." In *Research in Organizational Change and Development*, edited by R.W. Woodman and W.A. Pasmore, Vol. 7. Greenwich, CT: JAI Press, 1993.

Baumeister, Roy F., and Mark R. Leary. "The Need to Belong: Desire for Interpersonal Attachments as a Fundamental Human Motivation." *Psychological Bulletin* 117, no. 3 (1995): 497–529. https://doi.org/10.1037/0033-2909.117.3.497.

Bednar, Jeffrey S., Benjamin M. Galvin, Blake E. Ashforth, and Ella Hafermalz. "Putting Identification in Motion: A Dynamic View of Organizational Identification." *Organization Science (Providence, R.I.)* 31, no. 1 (2020): 200–222. https://doi.org/10.1287/orsc.2018.1276.

Beggan, James K. "On the Social Nature of Nonsocial Perception: The Mere Ownership Effect." *Journal of Personality and Social Psychology* 62, no. 2 (1992): 229–37.

Bernhard, Fabian, and Michael O'Driscoll. "Psychological Ownership in Small Family-Owned Businesses: Leadership Style and Nonfamily-Employees' Work Attitudes and Behaviors." *Group and Organization Management* 36, no. 3 (2011): 345–84.

Blanchard, Kenneth H. *Leading at a Higher Level: Blanchard on Leadership and Creating High Performing Organizations.* 1st Edition. Upper Saddle River, N.J.: Prentice Hall, 2007.

Blanchard, Kenneth H., Susan Fowler, and Laurence Hawkins. *Self-Leadership and the One Minute Manager: Discover the Magic of No Excuses!: Increasing Effectiveness through Situational Self Leadership.* 1st ed. New York: Morrow, 2005.

Blanchard, Kenneth H., Eunice Parisi-Carew, and Donald Carew. *The One Minute Manager Builds High Performing Teams: New and Revised Edition.* 1st ed. New York, N.Y.: Morrow, 2009.

Blanchard, Kenneth H., Patricia Zigarmi, and Drea Zigarmi. *Leadership and the One Minute Manager: Increasing Effectiveness through Situational Leadership.* 1st ed. New York: Morrow, 1985.

Blasi, Joseph, Richard Freeman, and Douglas Kruse. "Do Broad-Based Employee Ownership, Profit Sharing and Stock Options Help the Best Firms Do Even Better?" *British Journal of Industrial Relations* 54, no. 1 (2016): 55–82. https://doi.org/10.1111/bjir.12135.

Bradler, Christiane, Robert Dur, Susanne Neckermann, and Arjan Non. "Employee Recognition and Performance: A Field Experiment." *Management Science* 62, no. 11 (2016): 3085–99. https://doi.org/10.1287/mnsc.2015.2291.

Brown, Brené. *Dare to Lead: Brave Work. Tough Conversations. Whole Hearts.* New York: Random House, 2018.

Brown, Graham, Jon L. Pierce, and Craig Crossley. "Toward an Understanding of the Development of Ownership Feelings." *Journal of Organizational Behavior* 35 (2014): 318–38.

Chambers, Harry E. *My Way or the Highway: The Micromanagement Survival Guide.* Berrett-Koehler Publishers, 2004.

Chamorro-Premuzic, Tomas. "Does Money Really Affect Motivation? A Review of the Research." *Harvard Business Review* April 10 (2013).

Charan, Ram. *The Leadership Pipeline: How to Build the Leadership Powered Company*. 2nd ed. J-B US Non-Franchise Leadership. San Francisco, California: Jossey-Bass, 2011.

Chi, Nai-Wen, and Tzu-Shian Han. "Exploring the Linkages between Formal Ownership and Psychological Ownership for the Organization: The Mediating Role of Organizational Justice." *Journal of Occupational and Organizational Psychology* 81, no. 4 (2008): 691–711. https://doi.org/10.1348/096317907X262314.

Clear, James. *Atomic Habits: Tiny Changes, Remarkable Results: An Easy & Proven Way to Build Good Habits & Break Bad Ones*. New York, New York: Avery, an imprint of Penguin Random House, 2018.

Cleavenger, Dean J., and Timothy P. Munyon. "It's How You Frame It: Transformational Leadership and the Meaning of Work." *Business Horizons* 56, no. 3 (2013): 351–60. https://doi.org/10.1016/j.bushor.2013.01.002.

Colby, A., L. Sippola, and E. Phelps. "Social Responsibility and Paid Work in Contemporary American Life." In *Caring and Doing for Others: Social Responsibility in the Domains of Family, Work, and Community*, edited by A. Rossi, 349–99. Chicago: Chicago University Press, 2001.

Collins, James C. *Good to Great: Why Some Companies Make the Leap ... and Others Don't*. 1st ed. Business Book Summary. New York, NY: HarperBusiness, 2001.

Cram, F., and H. Paton. "Personal Possessions and Self-Identity: The Experiences of Elderly Women in Three Residential Settings." *Australian Journal of Aging* 12, no. 1 (1993): 19–24.

Dawkins, Sarah, Amy Wei Tian, Alexander Newman, and Angela Martin. "Psychological Ownership: A Review and Research Agenda." *Journal of Organizational Behavior* 38 (2017): 163–83.

Delgado, Osmel, Elaine Mebel Strauss, and Melissa A. Ortega. "Micromanagement: When to Avoid It and How to Use It Effectively." *American Journal of Health-System Pharmacy* 72, no. 10 (2015): 772–76. https://doi.org/10.2146/ajhp140125.

Demerouti, Evangelina. "Design Your Own Job Through Job Crafting." *European Psychologist* 19 (2014): 237–47.

Demsetz, Harold. "Toward a Theory of Property Rights." *American Economic Review* 62 (1967): 347–59.

Dittmar, Helga. *The Social Psychology of Material Possessions: To Have Is to Be.* New York: St. Martin's Press, 1992.

Dweck, Carol S. *Mindset: The New Psychology of Success.* Updated edition., Ballantine Books Trade Paperback edition. New York: Ballantine Books, 2016.

Edmondson, Amy C. *The Fearless Organization: Creating Psychological Safety in the Workplace for Learning, Innovation, and Growth.* Hoboken, N.J.: Wiley, 2019.

Edwards, Martin R. "Organizational Identification: A Conceptual and Operational Review." *International Journal of Management Reviews* 7, no. 4 (2005): 207–30. https://doi.org/10.1111/j.1468-2370.2005.00114.x.

Fairhurst, Gail Theus. *The Art of Framing: Managing the Language of Leadership.* 1st ed. Jossey-Bass Business & Management Series. San Francisco: Jossey-Bass Publishers, 1996.

Finnegan, Richard. *The Stay Interview: A Manager's Guide to Keeping the Best and Brightest.* 1st ed. Nashville: AMACOM, 2015.

Fonagy, Peter, Nicolas Lorenzini, Chloe Campbell, and Patrick Luyten. "Attachment and Personality Pathology." In *The Routledge Handbook of Attachment: Theory,* edited by Paul Holmes and Steve Farnland, 31–48. New York: Routledge, 2014.

Frederick, Donald E., and Tyler J. VanderWeele. "Longitudinal Meta-Analysis of Job Crafting Shows Positive Association with Work Engagement." *Cogent Psychology* 7, no. 1 (2020). https://doi.org/10.1080/23311908.2020.17 46733.

Friedman, Ori, Karen Neary, Margaret Defeyter, and Sarah Malcolm. "Ownership and Object History." In *Origins of Property Ownership,* 79–89. New Directions for Child and Adolescent Development 132. San Francisco: Wiley Periodicals, Inc., 2011.

Furby, Lita. "Understanding the Psychology of Possession and Ownership: A Personal Memoir and an Appraisal of Our Progress." *Journal of Social Behavior and Personality* 6 (1991): 457–63.

Giuliani, Maria Vittoria. "Theory of Attachment and Place Attachment." In *Psychological Theories for Environmental Issues,* 137–70. Aldershot: Ashgate, 2003.

Grant, Adam M. "Relational Job Design and the Motivation to Make a Prosocial Difference." *The Academy of Management Review* 32, no. 2 (2007): 393–417. https://doi.org/10.5465/AMR.2007.24351328.

———. "The Significance of Task Significance: Job Performance Effects, Relational Mechanisms, and Boundary Conditions."

Journal of Applied Psychology 93, no. 1 (2008): 108–24. https://doi.org/10.1037/0021-9010.93.1.108.

Hams, Brad. *Ownership Thinking: How to End Entitlement and Create a Culture of Accountability, Purpose, and Profit*. 1st edition. New York: McGraw-Hill, 2012.

Hansen, Stephen C., David T. Otley, and Wim A. Van der Stede. "Practice Developments in Budgeting: An Overview and Research Perspective." *Journal of Management Accounting Research* 15, no. 1 (2003): 95–116. https://doi.org/10.2308/jmar.2003.15.1.95.

Harcourt, Edward. "Attachment Theory, Character, and Naturalism." In *Aristotelian Ethics in Contemporary Perspective*, edited by Julia Peters, 145–57. Routledge Studies in Ethics and Moral Theory 21. New York: Routledge, 2013.

Harter, Jim. "Is Quiet Quitting Real?" *Gallup Workplace* (blog), May 17, 202AD. https://www.gallup.com/workplace/398306/quiet-quitting-real.aspx.

Hennig, Jan C., Carolin Ahrens, Jana Oehmichen, and Michael Wolff. "Employee Stock Ownership and Firm Exit Decisions: A Cross-Country Analysis of Rank-and-File Employees." *Accounting, Organizations and Society* 104 (2023): 101390-. https://doi.org/10.1016/j.aos.2022.101390.

Huang, Guo-hua, Ned Wellman, Susan J. Ashford, Cynthia Lee, and Li Wang. "Deviance and Exit: The Organizational Costs of Job Insecurity and Moral Disengagement." *Journal of Applied Psychology* 102, no. 1 (2017): 26–42. https://doi.org/10.1037/apl0000158.

Huang, Xu, Joyce Iun, Aili Liu, and Yaping Gong. "Does Participative Leadership Enhance Work Performance by Inducing Empowerment or Trust? The Differential Effects on Managerial and Non-Managerial Subordinates." *Journal of Organizational Behavior* 31, no. 1 (2010): 122–43. https://doi.org/10.1002/job.636.

Hume, David. *A Treatise of Human Nature*. Edited by David Norton and Mary Norton. Oxford: Oxford University Press, 2000.

———. *Essays, Moral, Political and Literary; An Enquiry Concerning the Principles of Morals*. Edited by T.H. Green and T.H. Grosse. London: Longmans, Green, and Co., 1898.

Irani-Williams, Feruzan, Lori Tribble, Paige S. Rutner, Constance Campbell, D. Harrison McKnight, and Bill C. Hardgrave. "Just Let Me Do My Job: Exploring the Impact of Micromanagement on IT Professionals." *ACM SIGMIS Database: The DATABASE for Advances in Information Systems* 52, no. 3 (2021): 77–95. https://doi.org/10.1145/3481629.3481635.

Jaeggi, Rahel. *Alienation*. Edited by Frederick Neuhouser. Translated by Frederick Neuhouser and Alan E. Smith. New York: Columbia University Press, 2014.

James, William. *The Principles of Psychology*. New York: Dover, 1890.

Jensen, M.C. "Corporate Budgeting Is Broken—Let's Fix It." *Harvard Business Review* 79, no. 10 (2001): 94–101.

Kalish, Charles, and Craig D. Anderson. "Ownership as a Social Status." In *Origins of Property Ownership*, 65–77. New Directions for Child and Adolescent Development 132. San Francisco: Wiley Periodicals, Inc., 2011.

Kanter, R.M. *Men and Women of the Corporation*. New York: Basic Books, 1977.

———. "The Middle Manager as Innovator." *Harvard Business Review* July-August (2004): 150–60.

Karabinski, Tina, Verena C. Haun, Annika Nübold, Johannes Wendsche, and Jürgen Wegge. "Interventions for Improving Psychological Detachment From Work: A Meta-Analysis." *Journal of Occupational Health Psychology* 26, no. 3 (2021): 224–42. https://doi.org/10.1037/ocp0000280.

Knapp, Joshua, Brett Smith, and Therese Sprinkle. "Clarifying the Relational Ties of Organizational Belonging: Understanding the Roles of Perceived Insider Status, Psychological Ownership, and Organizational Identification." *Journal of Leadership & Organizational Studies* 21, no. 3 (2014): 273–85.

Kopaneva, Irina, and Patricia M. Sias. "Lost in Translation: Employee and Organizational Constructions of Mission and Vision." *Management Communication Quarterly* 29, no. 3 (August 1, 2015): 358–84. https://doi.org/10.1177/0893318915581648.

Leary, Mark R., and Roy F. Baumeister. "The Nature and Function of Self-Esteem: Sociometer Theory." In *Advances in Experimental Social Psychology*, 32:1–62. United States: Academic Press, 2000. https://doi.org/10.1016/S0065-2601(00)80003-9.

Lee, Allan, Sara Willis, and Amy Wei Tian. "Empowering Leadership: A Meta-Analytic Examination of Incremental Contribution, Mediation, and Moderation." *Journal of Organizational Behavior* 39, no. 3 (2018): 306–25. https://doi.org/10.1002/job.2220.

Lee, Cynthia, Guo-Hua Huang, and Susan J. Ashford. "Job Insecurity and the Changing Workplace: Recent Developments and the Future Trends in Job Insecurity Research." *Annual Review of Organizational Psychology and Organizational Behavior* 5, no. 1 (2018): 335–59. https://doi.org/10.1146/annurev-orgpsych-032117-104651.

Lee, Sang Hyun, and Dae Yong Jeong. "Job Insecurity and Turnover Intention: Organizational Commitment as Mediator." *Social Behavior and Personality* 45, no. 4 (2017): 529–36. https://doi.org/10.2224/sbp.5865.

Lencioni, Patrick. *The Advantage: Why Organizational Health Trumps Everything Else in Business*. 1st ed. San Francisco: Jossey-Bass, 2012.

Lighthouse Research and Advisory. "Performance, Engagement, and Culture Enablement Study," 2023.

Liu, Jun, Hui Wang, Chun Hui, and Cynthia Lee. "Psychological Ownership: How Having Control Matters." *Journal of Management Studies,* 49, no. 5 (2012): 869–95.

Locke, John. *Two Treatises of Government*. Edited by L. A. Selby-Bigge. Oxford: Clarendon Press, 1739.

Mael, Fred A., and Lois E. Tetrick. "Identifying Organizational Identification. Educational and Psychological Measurement." *Educational and Psychological Measurement* 52, no. 4 (1992): 813–24.

Martinko, Mark J., and William L. Gardner. "Learned Helplessness: An Alternative Explanation for Performance Deficits." *The Academy of Management Review* 7, no. 2 (1982): 195–204. https://doi.org/10.5465/amr.1982.4285559.

Mayhew, Melissa G., Neal M. Ashkanasy, Tom Bramble, and John Gardner. "A Study of the Antecedents and Consequences of Psychological Ownership in Organizational Settings." *The Journal of Social Psychology* 147, no. 5 (2007): 477–500.

Mejia, Zameena. "Tech Workers Say This Is the Worst Trait a Boss Can Have.," 2018. https://www.cnbc.com/2018/03/26/tech-workers-say-this-is-the-worst-trait-a-boss-can-have.html.

Men, Linjuan Rita. "Strategic Internal Communication: Transformational Leadership, Communication Channels, and Employee Satisfaction." *Management Communication Quarterly* 28, no. 2 (2014): 264–84. https://doi.org/10.1177/0893318914524536.

Mészáros, István. *Marx's Theory of Alienation*. London: Merlin Press, 1970.

Mishra, Namrata, M Rajkumar, and Rajiv Mishra. "Micromanagement: An Employers' Perspective." *International Journal of Scientific & Technology Research* 8, no. 10 (2019): 2949–52.

Morrison, Elizabeth Wolfe. "Role Definitions and Organizational Citizenship Behavior: The Importance of the Employee's Perspective." *Academy of Management Journal* 37, no. 6 (1994): 1543–67.

Murray, Sandra L., John G. Holmes, and Dale W. Griffin. "The Benefits of Positive Illusions: Idealization and the Construction of Satisfaction in Close Relationships." *Journal of Personality and Social Psychology* 70, no. 1 (1996): 79–98. https://doi.org/10.1037/0022-3514.70.1.79.

— — —. "The Self-Fulfilling Nature of Positive Illusions in Romantic Relationships: Love Is Not Blind, but Prescient." *Journal of Personality and Social Psychology* 71, no. 6 (1996): 1155–80. https://doi.org/10.1037/0022-3514.71.6.1155.

National Lampoon's Christmas Vacation. Directed by Jeremiah S. Chechik. Burbank, CA: Warner Bros., 1989.

Oakley, Justin, and Dean Cocking. "Professional Detachment in Healthcare and Legal Practice." In *Virtue Ethics and Professional Roles.* Cambridge: Cambridge University Press, 2001.

Olafsen, Anja H., Hallgeir Halvari, Jacques Forest, and Edward L. Deci. "Show Them the Money? The Role of Pay, Managerial Need Support, and Justice in a Self-Determination Theory Model of Intrinsic Work Motivation." *Scandinavian Journal of Psychology* 56, no. 4 (2015): 447–57. https://doi.org/10.1111/sjop.12211.

Peck, Joann, and Webb Luangrath Andrea. "Looking Ahead: Future Research in Psychological Ownership." In *Psychological Ownership and Consumer Behavior*, edited by Joann Peck and Suzanne Shu. Springer, 2018.

Peng, He, and Jon Pierce. "Job- and Organization-Based Psychological Ownership: Relationship and Outcomes." *Journal of Managerial Psychology* 30, no. 2 (2015): 151–68.

Peterson, Christopher. *Learned Helplessness: A Theory for the Age of Personal Control.* New York: Oxford University Press, 1993.

Pierce, Jon L., and Iiro Jussila. *Psychological Ownership and the Organizational Context.* Northampton, MA: Edward Elgar Publishing, 2011.

Pierce, Jon L., Tatiana Kostova, and Kurt T. Dirks. "The State of Psychological Ownership: Integrating and Extending a Century of Research." *Review of General Psychology* 7, no. 1 (2003): 84–107.

— — —. "Toward a Theory of Psychological Ownership in Organizations." *The Academy of Management Review* 26, no. 2 (2001): 298–310.

Porteous, Douglas J. "Home: The Territorial Core." *Geographical Review* 66, no. 4 (1976): 383–90.

Roberts, Robert C. *Emotions: An Essay in Aid of Moral Psychology.* Cambridge; New York: Cambridge University Press, 2003.

— — —. *Emotions in the Moral Life.* Cambridge: Cambridge University Press, 2013.

Rochat, Philippe. *Origins of Possession: Owning and Sharing in Development.* Cambridge: Cambridge University Press, 2014.

———. "Possessions and Morality in Early Development." In *Origins of Property Ownership*, 23–38. New Directions for Child and Adolescent Development 132. San Francisco: Wiley Periodicals, Inc., 2011.

Rosen, Corey. *Beyond Engagement: How to Make Your Business an Idea Factory.* National Center for Employee Ownership, 2020.

Rousseau, Jean-Jacques. *Discourse on Inequality.* New York: Penguin Books, 1984.

Ryan, Richard M., and Edward L. Deci. "Self-Determination Theory and the Facilitation of Intrinsic Motivation, Social Development, and Well-Being." *The American Psychologist* 55, no. 1 (2000): 68–78. https://doi.org/10.1037/0003-066X.55.1.68.

Scannell, Leila, and Robert Gifford. "Defining Place Attachment: A Tripartite Organizing Framework." *Journal of Environmental Psychology* 30 (2010): 1–10.

Schnackenberg, Andrew K., and Edward C. Tomlinson. "Organizational Transparency: A New Perspective on Managing Trust in Organization-Stakeholder Relationships." *Journal of Management* 42, no. 7 (2016): 1784–1810. https://doi.org/10.1177/0149206314525202.

Schnatter, Kristin M., Jason J. Dahling, and Samantha L. Chau. "Examining Career Pathing Through the Lens of Identity Theories." In *Identity as a Foundation for Human Resource Development*, 1st ed., 53–65. Routledge, 2018. https://doi.org/10.4324/9781315671482-4.

Sinek, Simon. *Start with WHY: How Great Leaders Inspire Everyone to Take Action.* New York: Portfolio, 2009.

Sonnentag, Sabine, Carmen Binnewies, and Eva J. Mojza. "Staying Well and Engaged When Demands Are High: The Role of Psychological Detachment." *Journal of Applied Psychology* 95, no. 5 (2010): 965–76. https://doi.org/10.1037/a0020032.

Sonnentag, Sabine, and Caterina Schiffner. "Psychological Detachment from Work during Nonwork Time and Employee Well-Being: The Role of Leader's Detachment." *The Spanish Journal of Psychology* 22 (2019): E3–E3. https://doi.org/10.1017/sjp.2019.2.

Stanier, Michael Bungay. *The Coaching Habit.* 1st edition. Page Two, 2016.

Steed, Laurens Bujold, Brian W. Swider, Sejin Keem, and Joseph T. Liu. "Leaving Work at Work: A Meta-Analysis on Employee Recovery

From Work." *Journal of Management* 47, no. 4 (2021): 867–97. https://doi.org/10.1177/0149206319864153.

Unanue, Wenceslao, Marcos Esteban Gomez Mella, Diego Alejandro Cortez, Diego Bravo, Claudio Araya-Véliz, Jesús Unanue, and Anja Van Den Broeck. "The Reciprocal Relationship Between Gratitude and Life Satisfaction: Evidence From Two Longitudinal Field Studies." *Frontiers in Psychology* 10 (2019): 2480–2480. https://doi.org/10.3389/fpsyg.2019.02480.

Van Dyne, Linn, and Jon L. Pierce. "Psychological Ownership and Feelings of Possession: Three Field Studies Predicting Employee Attitudes and Organizational Citizenship Behavior." *Journal of Organizational Behavior* 25 (2004): 439–359.

VandeWalle, Don, Linn Van Dyne, and Tatiana Kostova. "Psychological Ownership: An Empirical Examination of Its Consequences." *Group & Organization Management* 20, no. 2 (1995): 210–26.

Weisman, Hannah, Chia-Huei Wu, Katsuhiko Yoshikawa, and Hyun-Jung Lee. "Antecedents of Organizational Identification: A Review and Agenda for Future Research." *Journal of Management* 49, no. 6 (2023): 2030–61. https://doi.org/10.1177/01492063221140049.

Weltmann, Dan, Joseph Blasi, and Douglas Kruse. *At What Threshold Do Employee Shares Have a Meaningful Effect?* New Brunswick, NJ: Rutgers University School of Management and Labor Relations, 2013.

White, Richard D. "The Micromanagement Disease: Symptoms, Diagnosis, and Cure." *Public Personnel Management* 39, no. 1 (2010): 71–76. https://doi.org/10.1177/009102601003900105.

Willink, Jocko, and Leif Babin. *Extreme Ownership: How U.S. Navy SEALs Lead and Win.* New York: St. Martin's Press, 2015.

Wilms, Lisa. "What Ownership in the Workplace Means to Me." *InfoTrust* (blog), March 24, 2017. https://infotrust.com/articles/what-ownership-in-the-workplace-means-to-me/.

Wilson, Matthew F. "The Virtue of Taking Ownership." ProQuest Dissertations Publishing, 2018. https://search.proquest.com/docview/2054314035.

Wong, Kenman L., and Scott B. Rae. *Business for the Common Good: A Christian Vision for the Marketplace.* Downers Grove, Ill: IVP Academic, 2011.

Wrzesniewski, Amy, and Jane Dutton. "Crafting a Job: Revisioning Employees as Active Crafters of Their Work." *Academy of Management Review* 26 (2001): 179–201.

Wrzesniewski, Amy, Nicholas LoBuglio, Jane Dutton, and Justin Berg. "Job Crafting and Cultivating Positive Meaning and Identity in Work." *Advances in Positive Organizational Psychology* 1 (2013): 281–302.

Yeager, David S., Paul Hanselman, Gregory M. Walton, Jared S. Murray, Robert Crosnoe, Chandra Muller, and Elizabeth Tipton. "A National Experiment Reveals Where a Growth Mindset Improves Achievement." *Nature* 573, no. 7774 (2019): 364–69. https://doi.org/10.1038/s41586-019-1466-y.

Zhu, Hang, Chao C. Chen, Xinchun Li, and Yinghui Zhou. "From Personal Relationship to Psychological Ownership: The Importance of Manager–Owner Relationship Closeness in Family Businesses." *Management and Organization Review* 9, no. 2 (2013): 295–318.